£1-50

MEDITERRANEAN VEGETARIAN COOKING

Join Colin Spencer on a culinary voyage which takes in traditional favourites and original variations — all redolent with the flavour and atmosphere of this much-loved region.

Leoni

D1386651

By the same author
CORDON VERT

MEDITERRANEAN VEGETARIAN COOKING

COLIN SPENCER

THORSONS PUBLISHING GROUP
Wellingborough • New York

Published in the UK by Thorsons Publishers Ltd., Denington Estate, Wellingborough, Northamptonshire NN8 2RQ, and in the USA by Thorsons Publishers Inc., 377 Park Avenue South, New York, NY 10016. Thorsons Publishers Inc. are distributed to the trade by Inner Traditions International Ltd., New York.

First published 1986

Library of Congress Cataloging-in-Publication Data

Spencer, Colin.
  Mediterranean vegetarian cooking.

  Includes index.
  1. Vegetarian cookery. 2. Cookery, Mediterranean.
  I. Title.
  TX837.S688 1986   641.5′636′091822   86-1419

  ISBN 0-7225-0979-0 (pbk.)

British Library Cataloguing in Publication Data

Spencer, Colin
  Mediterranean vegetarian cooking.
  1. Vegetarian cookery 2. Cookery, Mediterranean
  I. Title
  641.5′636′091822   TX837

  ISBN 0 7225 0979 0

Printed and Bound in Great Britain by
Whitstable Litho Ltd., Whitstable, Kent

Contents

Introduction

The countries of the Mediterranean comprise the two provinces of southern France, Languedoc and Provence, though one cannot draw a neat line as their cooking is more and more influenced by other provinces: Corsica, Spain and the Balearic Islands, Gibraltar, North Africa (Morocco, Algeria, Tunisia, Libya and Egypt), those Middle Eastern countries that border the sea, Israel and Lebanon, then Turkey and Greece and all those islands that still bear the influence of Turkey in their cooking. Cyprus, which is partitioned and governed by both countries must be included here, too; the whole of Italy, Sicily and Sardinia. I have also included the tiny islands of Malta and Gozo, for though their cuisine suffered, I fear, from the domination of the British for 150 years, a few inherently traditional Maltese dishes have survived.

Is there anything that unites this polyglot collection apart from the Mediterranean sea, which appears if you look at these countries more like an inland lake, and the climatic conditions of hot dry summers and rumbustious cold and wet winters, conditions dictated by the Sahara desert and the Atlantic ocean? Amazingly enough, though the countries differ widely in faith and economics and in history and politics, the soil conditions are not so dissimilar and the crops grown tend to be much the same — though what is done with them is another story.

What distinguishes this geographical area for me in its cuisine are three basic crops: the olive and its oil, the garlic and the tomato. The latter is a newcomer, being one of the plants brought back from the New World, but it very quickly became popular, especially in Spain and Italy where it flourished (workmen eating their tomatoes for lunch and spitting out the seeds is a common sight; I have often noticed that the following spring the tomato plants will be growing from those same spots) and now we cannot think of Mediterranean cuisine without the tomato, its paste and its sauces.

But it is the olive and its oil that has so radically influenced the cooking of this area, largely because the poverty of the soil allows no pasture and hence no dairy herds. Cream, milk and butter are not produced and the oil from the olive has been used instead. We know that because this oil is high in monosaturated and low in polyunsaturated and saturated fats, the olive oil is neutral and does not induce a tendency to fur the arteries and increase the chance of a coronary. Hence the cooking of this large and varied area is consistently healthy. We also know that garlic has an immensely beneficial influence on health; large amounts of it eaten over a short period can begin to halt the furring of the arteries and the risk of coronary heart attacks is thus lowered. I mention the health aspect in passing because it is good to be aware of it, especially when the cuisine itself is so magnificently delicious in its own right.

I have travelled the area in the last thirty years, sometimes pausing to live on a Greek island, in Sicily or the coast of Italy or France long enough to learn to shop and know some of the details of the local markets. I have also grown my own vegetables in some of these areas, battling against stony soil which in many cases only covered the rock beneath by 10 inches or so. I dug despairingly at it, thinking that it was too parched and poor to grow a thing, but after those heavy rains that start in January, suddenly in late April the earth is alive with wild flowers, with anemones, orchids and lilies, with the flowers of the caper bush that so resemble a flight of birds of paradise. And then you plant a seed and within a few days it is showing a green tip. All of my Mediterranean gardens flourished if they had their daily watering; their produce was cooked following methods and recipes which I had gathered from local friends.

The other triumph of the Mediterranean is its herbs. The purple flowers of the thyme grow from cracks in the rock on the mountains but if you take an observant stroll you can find wild mints, sage and rosemary. I have picked kilos of oregano in Greece. I have found wild garlic in Provence, though one would not want to use it when the cultivated garlic can be found in the markets at such plump and gargantuan size.

What is not found on or near your doorstep can be purchased at the market — pots of bush basil or bouquets of their leaves are always sold from one stall, often with a couple of ropes of garlic, a few lemons and some tomatoes, for it is the produce from one small garden. Because these herbs grow high up in the mountains, in sun-scorched areas, they are more intense in flavour than if cultivated in shady and watered places. It is this intensity of herb and spice that gives the regional cooking its great kick.

The Mediterranean vegetarian tradition is both rich and ancient for two reasons: religious and economic. In those countries where Catholicism rules, there were rich feast days and there were the days of Lent where meat was eschewed and very often fish as well. The more dull your diet the more the piety showed, yet humanity, being its own inconsistent self, could not face dull dishes for long. So given the simple materials (vegetables, eggs and cheeses), dishes would be created having more style and flair than was perhaps suitable for a devout creature. Torta Pasqualina is one that springs to mind, looking more like a wedding cake than a vegetable pie. As to economics, these peoples for centuries have been poor and feudal, for the most part making their living off the land and out of the sea. It would be rare to eat meat, for to slaughter an animal was to kill off capital. As to fish, long winter storms in this fickle and treacherous sea can destroy the living of a

8

fisherman sometimes for weeks on end, and then the diet falls back on the salting of fish or plain vegetables, bread, cheese and grains including rice. Now of course the diet is supplemented by tinned or canned foods. It is sadly true that in the primitive and less habitable parts of Greece and Italy (where the dried bean should rule) I have seen housewives buying tins of baked beans, and my heart has sunk.

The pulse family is another great richness of this area and nearly all the great bean dishes come from the Mediterranean (I grant you that there are single dishes from Mexico, the Caribbean and China). The bean mixes well with the thick, green olive oil from the first pressing, with the juice of garlic, with thyme and rosemary, and that mixture with the addition of water can make one of the best soups in the world. It is this diet which can be considered by the people themselves to be the most modest one, but which we can take a new look at and see for ourselves that there is great richness in the simplicity of it. For though there are no thick butters, creams and high-fat cheeses, there are marvellous tangy cheeses made from goat's milk and hard cheese which grated into soups and over pasta provide the perfect accompaniment.

It is also a diet that because of the import of so many of its foods into Northern Europe and the Americas we can easily adopt. I think, on the whole, it is the best diet in the world. The dishes are simple to concoct, varied because of the use of herbs and spices and always stimulating to the palate. Besides, the smell of them when cooking takes me back to the Greek mountains and Sicilian seas, when body and soul were at peace and for a moment or two the harsh winds and depressing dampness of my own native climate be banished.

When red kidney beans are used in a recipe, they should after being soaked, be boiled fiercely for 10 minutes and the water thrown away, then the cooking resumed.

No one could write today about Mediterranian cooking without a heavy debt of gratitude to the life work of Elizabeth David. No one could ignore either the writings of Claudia Roden, who brought the whole range of Middle Eastern cooking out of obscurity twenty years ago. Latterly, there have also been noted works by Arabella Boxer, David Scott and Arto der Haroutunian on the subject. My sincere thanks to them all, for they have helped me to check sources and jar the palate's memory so that I have rediscovered dishes for this book I first cooked and ate thirty years ago.

Chapter 1
Appetizers, Mezzés and Tapas

In the Mediterranean it is the tradition to nibble at various delights while taking the evening drink. In Spain and Greece these offerings can often be so numerous and delicious that they become, in fact, the first course of the meal.

One or several of these purées with fresh vegetables, eaten *au naturel* as crudités, could be the best way of starting a summer meal.

AUBERGINE (EGGPLANT) PURÉE

Greece

Imperial (Metric)	American
2 lb (900g) aubergines	2 pounds eggplant
4 tablespoons olive oil	4 tablespoons olive oil
2 tablespoons lemon juice	2 tablespoons lemon juice
3 cloves crushed garlic,	3 crushed cloves garlic,
sea salt and black pepper	sea salt and black pepper

1

Grill the aubergines (eggplant) so that the skin is blackened and can be flaked off. This will give the flesh a charred and smoky flavour which is necessary. If you have a charcoal grill, they can be barbecued until they are soft inside, about 30 minutes. If you are using a grill continue to cook them until the flesh is soft.

2

Let them cool. Peel off all the outside skin. Then put all the flesh into a blender and purée with the other ingredients. Chill a few hours before serving so that the oil thickens. Serve with hot pitta bread or brown toast.

SESAME AUBERGINE (EGGPLANT)

Egypt

Add 2 oz (55g or about $\frac{1}{2}$ cup) roasted sesame seeds to the above ingredients and sprinkle a little more on the top. Roast the seeds by putting them into a dry pan, covered. Shake the pan a few minutes over a flame until the seeds have turned gold and give off the delicious aroma of sesame oil.

SPICED AUBERGINE (EGGPLANT) PURÉE

Turkey

Add a tablespoon of garam masala to the sesame aubergine.

AUBERGINE (EGGPLANT) PURÉE II

Italy

Instead of olive oil, use 5 fl oz (150ml or $\frac{2}{3}$ cup) sour cream or yogurt and a dash of Tabasco.

AUBERGINE (EGGPLANT) PURÉE III

Italy

Add 4 peeled tomatoes finely chopped and one green pepper, also chopped, to the first recipe. And if you like it hot, use a dash of Tabasco.

IMAM BAYELDI
The Imam Fainted

Turkey

Imperial (Metric)	American
3 aubergines	3 eggplants
3 peppers	3 peppers
5 cloves garlic, crushed	5 cloves garlic, crushed
½ lb (225g) onions, sliced	1⅓ cups sliced onions
5 fl oz (150ml) olive oil	⅔ cup olive oil
1 lb (450g) tomatoes	1 pound tomatoes
sea salt and black pepper	sea salt and black pepper

1
Hold the aubergines (eggplant) over a naked flame or place under a hot grill to burn and blister the outer skin. This is best done over a barbecue to get the charcoal flavour. But the burning and blistering, however it is done, is necessary to the dish. Scrape off and discard the outer skin, pour a little of the olive oil over the flesh and bake in a preheated 400F/200C (Gas Mark 6) oven 20 minutes or until the interior flesh is cooked through.

2
Meanwhile place the sliced peppers, crushed garlic and onions in the rest of the olive oil in a pan and cook 15 to 20 minutes. Skin the tomatoes and add them. Season and continue to cook another 10 minutes.

3
Stir in the aubergine (eggplant) flesh. Let it cool. Place in the blender to make a smooth purée. Serve cool with warm pitta bread.

CRUDITÉS

France

This is the best appetizer of all, especially in the Mediterranean countries where the range of fresh vegetables is larger and more varied than what is readily available elsewhere.

Presenting the crudités is a little like arranging flowers. It must look spectacular and enticing. Use fresh vegetables at their peak, pick them young and slice them so they are easy to handle. Aim for different colour combinations. Use peppers, fennel, courgettes (zucchini), celery, green beans, spring onions (scallions), radishes, cucumbers, tomatoes and kohlrabi. Serve some of the purées and a mayonnaise with them.

BROAD BEANS IN THEIR PODS

Greece

Young broad beans are served in their pods with ouzo, cubes of bread, sea salt and other mezzé.

They are served like this in Provence and southern Italy.

GIGANTES SALATA
Butter (Lima) Bean Salad

Greece

Imperial (Metric)	American
$\frac{1}{2}$ lb (225g) butter beans	$1\frac{1}{3}$ cups lima beans
1 bunch spring onions, chopped	1 bunch scallions, chopped
5 cloves garlic, crushed	5 cloves garlic, crushed
12 black olives, stoned and halved	12 black olives, pitted and halved
juice and zest of 2 lemons	juice and zest of 2 lemons
5 fl oz (150ml) olive oil	$\frac{2}{3}$ cup olive oil
sea salt and black pepper	sea salt and black pepper
2 tablespoons each chopped parsley and mint	2 tablespoons each chopped parsley and mint

1

Soak the beans overnight then boil them 1 hour or until tender.

2

Drain the beans and pour them into a bowl with the rest of the ingredients and mix well.

FASOLIA MAVROMITIKA
Black-eyed Bean Salad

Greece

Follow the preceding recipe but use black-eyed beans which will need less cooking — about 30 minutes.

KOUNOUPITHI SALATA
Cauliflower Salad

Greece

Imperial (Metric)	American
1 large cauliflower	1 large cauliflower
5 tablespoons olive oil	5 tablespoons olive oil
2 teaspoons dried oregano	2 teaspoons dried oregano
juice and zest of 1 lemon	juice and zest of 1 lemon
5 crushed cloves garlic	5 crushed cloves garlic
sea salt and black pepper	sea salt and black pepper

1

Cut the cauliflower into its florets and boil them in a little salted water 4–5 minutes so that they are just tender but still al dente.

2

Drain the cauliflower well. Pour the oil into a frying pan and add the dried oregano. Let the herb cook for a moment to release its fragrance.

3

Put the lemon juice and zest into a large bowl with the crushed cloves of garlic, add the salt and pepper and the oil and oregano. Mix well.

4

Add the cauliflower to the bowl and toss the salad thoroughly.

DOLMADES
Stuffed Vine Leaves

Greece

Imperial (Metric)	American
½ lb (225g) drained vine leaves	½ pound drained vine leaves
½ lb (225g) uncooked brown rice	1 cup uncooked brown rice
2 finely chopped onions	2 finely chopped onions
4–5 crushed cloves garlic	4–5 crushed cloves garlic
2 tablespoons finely chopped celery leaves	2 tablespoons finely chopped celery leaves
1 teaspoon each crushed dill, thyme and oregano	1 teaspoon each crushed dill thyme and oregano
sea salt and black pepper	sea salt and black pepper
5 fl oz (150ml) olive oil	⅔ cup olive oil
juice of 2 lemons	juice of 2 lemons

1

Scald the rice in boiling water for a few seconds then rinse under cold water. Add the onions, garlic, celery, herbs and seasoning. Place a teaspoon of this mixture in the centre of each vine leaf, roll the leaf over the filling, tucking in the sides as you go.

2

In a thick-bottomed pan lay some outside leaves of cabbage, which will cushion the dolmades so that they will neither stick nor burn. Pack the stuffed vine leaves in so they are wedged together in a layer.

3

Pour in the olive oil and lemon juice with enough water to rise 2 or 3 inches (5–8cm) above the dolmades. Cook slowly over gentle heat 1½ to 2 hours.

4

Leave to cool in their own stock. They are splendid eaten chilled but can be reheated.

ESCALIBADA

Spain

Imperial (Metric)	American
1 lb (450g) aubergines	1 pound eggplant
1 lb (450g) mixed red, green and yellow peppers	1 pound mixed red, green and yellow peppers
12 black olives, stoned and halved	12 black olives, pitted and halved
5 crushed cloves garlic	5 crushed cloves garlic
4 tablespoons olive oil	4 tablespoons olive oil
1 tablespoon lemon juice	1 tablespoon lemon juice
sea salt and black pepper	sea salt and black pepper
2 tablespoons chopped parsley	2 tablespoons chopped parsley

1
Grill the aubergines (eggplant), blackening and blistering the skin. Let them cook thoroughly 15 to 20 minutes. Leave to cool.

2
Grill the peppers in the same manner (they will be cooked within 5 minutes). Leave to cool.

3
Cut the flesh of the vegetables into strips, discarding the seeds from the peppers. Lay them in alternate layers on a platter.

4
Sprinkle with the black olives. Make a dressing with the garlic, olive oil, lemon juice and seasoning. Pour dressing over the vegetables and sprinkle with parsley.

RABANOS
White Radishes

Spain

Imperial (Metric)	American
3–4 long white radishes	3 to 4 long white radishes
2 oz (55g) butter	$\frac{1}{4}$ cup butter
1 teaspoon cayenne pepper	1 teaspoon cayenne pepper
sea salt	sea salt

1

Clean and trim the radishes then slice them diagonally.

2

Smear a little butter on each slice and sprinkle with cayenne pepper and sea salt.

CHALOTAS CON ACEITUNAS
Shallots and Olives

Spain

Imperial (Metric)	American
$\frac{1}{2}$ lb (225g) shallots	$\frac{1}{2}$ pound shallots
10 stoned green and black olives	10 pitted green and black olives
1 tablespoon olive oil	1 tablespoon olive oil
1 tablespoon parsley	1 tablespoon parsley
sea salt and black pepper	sea salt and black pepper
2 tablespoons wholemeal breadcrumbs	2 tablespoons wholewheat breadcrumbs

1

Peel the shallots and boil them in a little salted water about 10 minutes; drain them well.

2

Mix them in a bowl with the rest of the ingredients.

TOMATES RELLENOS
Stuffed Tomatoes

Spain

Imperial (Metric)	American
6 tomatoes	6 tomatoes
2 hard-boiled eggs, peeled and chopped	2 hard-boiled eggs, peeled and chopped
2 tablespoons grated Manchego cheese	2 tablespoons grated Manchego cheese
2 tablespoons chopped parsley	2 tablespoons chopped parsley
1 teaspoon red wine vinegar	1 teaspoon red wine vinegar
1 tablespoon olive oil	1 tablespoon olive oil
sea salt and black pepper	sea salt and black pepper

1
Slice the tomatoes in half and cut out the pulp. Place pulp in a bowl leaving the empty shells.

2
Add the rest of the ingredients to the bowl and mix well. Spoon the stuffing into the tomato shells and chill before serving.

Note:
If Manchego cheese is unavailable, mature Cheddar can be substituted.

BOLITAS DE PATATA
Potato Fritters

Spain

Imperial (Metric)	American
2 lb (900g) potatoes	2 pounds potatoes
2 oz (55g) grated Manchego cheese	½ cup grated Manchego cheese
1 egg, beaten	1 egg, beaten
1 oz (30g) wholemeal flour	¼ cup whole wheat flour
sea salt and black pepper	sea salt and black pepper
corn oil for frying	corn oil for frying

1

Peel the potatoes and boil until tender in salted water. Drain them well.
Mash them with the cheese, egg, flour and seasoning.

2

Shape the mixture into balls and deep fry them in hot oil.

BLACK OLIVES

Greece

Fill a jar with black olives drained of their brine. Add a tablespoon of dried
oregano. Peel 5 or 6 cloves of garlic, slice thinly, and poke down amongst
the olives. Fill the jar with strong olive oil, cover the jar and leave several
weeks.

SKORDALIA I

Greece

Imperial (Metric)	American
1 lb (450g) floury potatoes	1 pound floury (Eastern) potatoes
5 crushed cloves garlic	5 crushed cloves garlic
2 egg yolks	2 egg yolks
5 fl oz (150ml) olive oil	$\frac{2}{3}$ cup olive oil
juice and zest of 1 lemon	juice and zest of 1 lemon
sea salt and black pepper	sea salt and black pepper

1
Peel and boil the potatoes, mash them and force them through a sieve.

2
Add the garlic, stir in the egg yolks and add the olive oil, drop by drop, until you have a thick purée. Taste for seasoning.

SKORDALIA II

Greece

Imperial (Metric)	American
2 egg yolks	2 egg yolks
5 fl oz (150ml) olive oil	⅔ cup olive oil
2 oz (55g) ground almonds	½ cup ground almonds
2 oz (55g) fresh wholemeal breadcrumbs	1 cup fresh wholewheat breadcrumbs
5 cloves crushed garlic	5 cloves crushed garlic
2 tablespoons chopped parsley	2 tablespoons chopped parsley
1 tablespoon lemon juice	1 tablespoon lemon juice
sea salt and black pepper	sea salt and black pepper

1

Place the egg yolks in a bowl and add the olive oil, drop by drop, as if making mayonnaise. Stir in the almonds and breadcrumbs, then the garlic, parsley and lemon juice. Season to taste. Splendid if eaten with warm pitta bread.

ENSALADA DE REMOLACHA
Beetroot Salad

Spain

Peel several boiled beetroots (beets), cut into thin slices and add a little wine vinegar and a lot of hot chilli oil. Garnish with sliced red pimentoes.

HUMMUS

Greece

Imperial (Metric)	American
6 oz (170g) chickpeas	$\frac{3}{4}$ cup chickpeas
4 crushed cloves garlic	4 crushed cloves garlic
juice and zest of 1 lemon	juice and zest of 1 lemon
5 fl oz (150ml) olive oil	$\frac{2}{3}$ cup olive oil
handful chopped mint	handful chopped mint
sea salt and black pepper	sea salt and black pepper

1
Soak the chickpeas overnight.

2
Boil them in water 2 hours; they are done when the point of a knife parts them. Chickpeas never disintegrate like other pulses.

3
Drain the chickpeas but save at least 5 fl oz (150ml) water.

4
Mix the peas in the blender with the rest of the ingredients to form a thick cream. If too thick, add some of the water the peas were cooked in.

FALAFEL

Israel

These are tiny cakes made from chickpeas. Use the purée above but without the olive oil. Add $\frac{1}{2}$ teaspoon baking powder, ground cumin and ground coriander. Also add 2 large onions finely chopped, sea salt and a good pinch of cayenne pepper. Pound everything into a smooth paste, mould into small cakes and shallow-fry in vegetable oil.

TAPENADE

France

Imperial (Metric)	American
4 oz (100g) black olives, stoned	1 cup black olives, stoned
2 oz (55g) capers	$\frac{1}{2}$ cup capers
4 crushed cloves garlic	4 crushed cloves garlic
5 fl oz (150ml) olive oil	$\frac{2}{3}$ cup olive oil
2 tablespoons fine breadcrumbs	2 tablespoons fine breadcrumbs

Blend all ingredients together into a thick cream.

LENTIL PURÉE

Egypt

Imperial (Metric)	American
$\frac{1}{2}$ lb (225g) cooked lentils	1 cup cooked lentils
2 crushed cloves garlic	2 crushed cloves garlic
1 tablespoon lemon juice	1 tablespoon lemon juice
3 tablespoons olive oil	3 tablespoons olive oil
2 oz (55g) fine wholemeal breadcrumbs, fresh	1 cup fine whole wheat breadcrumbs, fresh
sea salt and black pepper	sea salt and black pepper
handful of chopped chives or parsley	handful of chopped chives or parsley

Place all ingredients in a blender and mix to a thick cream.

FALAFEL II

Egypt

These are made with the lentil purée on the previous page. Add a tablespoon of sieved gram flour (made from chickpeas and available from Indian shops). Add 1 beaten egg, mould into cakes and shallow fry in vegetable oil.

TAHINA CREAM

Turkey

Imperial (Metric)	American
5 fl oz (150ml) tahina paste	$\frac{2}{3}$ cup tahina paste
3 crushed cloves garlic	3 crushed cloves garlic
$\frac{1}{4}$ pint (150ml) lemon juice	$\frac{2}{3}$ cup lemon juice
$\frac{1}{2}$ teaspoon ground cumin	$\frac{1}{2}$ teaspoon ground cumin
$\frac{1}{2}$ teaspoon ground coriander	$\frac{1}{2}$ teaspoon ground coriander
sea salt and black pepper	sea salt and black pepper

Mix all the ingredients together in a blender. Eat with pitta bread.

ALMOND TAHINA CREAM

Lebanon

Omit the spices, but use the rest of the ingredients above, adding 2 oz (55g or $\frac{1}{2}$ cup) ground almonds and 2 oz (55g or $\frac{1}{2}$ cup) blanched almonds. Decorate the cream with more blanched almonds.

Alternative: A variation on this cream is to use crushed and broken walnuts instead of almonds.

27

TAHINA AND YOGURT

Tunisia

Imperial (Metric)	American
5 fl oz (150ml) tahina paste	$\frac{2}{3}$ cup tahina paste
$\frac{1}{4}$ pint (150ml) yogurt	$\frac{2}{3}$ cup yogurt
juice of 2 lemons	juice of 2 lemons
3 crushed cloves garlic	3 crushed cloves garlic
sea salt and black pepper	sea salt and black pepper

Mix all ingredients to a smooth paste in a blender.

BABA GHANOUSH

Turkey

Imperial (Metric)	American
$\frac{1}{2}$ pint (285ml) tahina paste	$1\frac{1}{3}$ cups tahina paste
3 large aubergines	3 large eggplants
5 crushed cloves garlic	5 crushed cloves garlic
5 fl oz (150ml) lemon juice	$\frac{2}{3}$ cup lemon juice
$\frac{1}{2}$ teaspoon ground cumin	$\frac{1}{2}$ teaspoon ground cumin
$\frac{1}{2}$ teaspoon ground coriander	$\frac{1}{2}$ teaspoon ground coriander
sea salt and black pepper	sea salt and black pepper

To get the authentic flavour, the aubergines (eggplants) should be cooked over charcoal, but it is almost the same if the outside skin is blistered and blackened over a gas flame or under a grill.

1

Grill the aubergines (eggplants) until the interior is soft and the exterior of the skin is blackened.

2

Slice them in half and to the cooked flesh add the rest of the ingredients, keeping the tahina paste until last. For a smoother cream use an electric blender.

GRILLED CHEESE

Cyprus

Haloumi is the Cypriot equivalent of Parmesan. It is a hard, salty cheese that can be sliced and then grilled. It is a perfect appetizer, but it must be cooked at the last minute, just before serving.

KEFALOTYRI SAGANAKI

Cyprus

Similar to Haloumi, Kefalotyri is a cheese that is often used grated with pasta and sauces. The cheese is cut in about $\frac{1}{4}$-inch (6mm) slices, dusted in flour and fried in oil until the slices turn brown.

Chapter 2
Hors d'Oeuvres and Light First Courses

Globe artichokes

Where globe artichokes are plentiful, as they are in all the Mediterranean countries, the leaves are discarded and the hearts and bottoms only are cooked and eaten in various ways. However, in France, Italy and Spain, the whole of the globe artichoke is boiled and eaten; the edible base of each leaf is dipped in sauce vinaigrette or melted butter.

Boiling the artichokes

Cut the sharp tips of the leaves away, trim the base so that it stands firmly on a flat surface and immerse in boiling salted water. Allow 1 artichoke per person. Depending on their size, they will need 20 to 40 minutes. They are done when the leaves are plucked easily from their base. They can be served hot, warm or chilled. They are generally eaten cold with a strong garlicky vinaigrette.

ALCACHOFA RELLENAS
Stuffed Artichokes

Spain

Allow 1 artichoke per person. Cook the artichokes, let them cool, and extract and discard the central leaves and choke. Mix finely chopped spring onions (scallions), capers and a little freshly made tomato purée with curd (cottage) or cream cheese. Stuff the artichokes with this mixture, chill and serve.

FARCIS D'ARTICHAUT
Stuffed Artichokes II

France

Allow 1 artichoke per person. Make a purée out of 1 pound (450g) freshly cooked broad beans by putting them in a blender with a carton of sour cream, a tablespoon of freshly chopped summer savory and seasoning. After discarding the centre as above, fill the artichokes with this purée, chill and serve.

FRICASSÉE D'ARTICHAUT
Fricassee of Artichoke Bottoms

France

Imperial (Metric)	American
12 cooked artichoke bottoms	12 cooked artichoke bottoms
6 oz (170g) butter	$\frac{2}{3}$ cup butter
$\frac{1}{2}$ pint (285ml) thick cream	$1\frac{1}{3}$ cups heavy cream
1 teaspoon lemon juice	1 teaspoon lemon juice
handful of chopped fresh parsley	handful of chopped fresh parsley
and tarragon	and tarragon
seasoning	seasoning

1
Cut the artichoke bottoms into $\frac{1}{2}$-inch (1.2cm) chunks and keep them warm.

2
Melt the butter in a pan, add the cream and stir until it is a thick sauce. Pour in the lemon juice and add the herbs and seasoning.

3
Add the artichoke pieces and pour into a serving dish.

GRILLADE D'ARTICHAUT POIVRÉ
Devilled Artichokes

France

Imperial (Metric)	American
12 cooked artichoke bottoms	12 cooked artichoke bottoms
1 tablespoon Dijon mustard	1 tablespoon Dijon mustard
$\frac{1}{2}$ pint (285ml) single cream	$1\frac{1}{3}$ cups light cream
dash of Tabasco	dash of Tabasco
sea salt and black pepper	sea salt and black pepper

1

Place the cooked bottoms in an earthenware dish and keep warm.

2

Mix the rest of the ingredients together; pour them over the artichokes.

3

Place under a hot grill until bubbling and slightly brown.

ANGINARES À LA POLITA

Artichokes Constantinople-style

Turkey and Greece

Imperial (Metric)	American
6 globe artichokes	6 globe artichokes
juice of 1 lemon	juice of 1 lemon
2 large onions	2 large onions
3–4 small carrots	3 to 4 small carrots
½ lb (225g) small new potatoes	½ pound small new potatoes
5 fl oz (150ml) olive oil	⅔ cup olive oil
3 tablespoons fresh dill	3 tablespoons fresh dill
½ pint (285g) water	1⅓ cups water
sea salt and black pepper	sea salt and black pepper

1

Take all the leaves from the artichoke, pull out the centre and cut away the choke. Trim the stalk so that you have 6 artichoke bottoms. Place these in a bowl of cold water with the lemon juice while you prepare the vegetables.

2

Slice the onions and carrots, wash and scrape the potatoes. Pour the olive oil into a pan and add the onions, carrots and dill. Cook 2-3 minutes. Add the potatoes and artichoke bottoms, the water and seasoning.

3

Simmer over low heat about 40 minutes. This dish may be eaten warm or chilled.

CARCIOFO E INSALATA DI PATATE
Artichoke Heart and Potato Salad

Italy

This is a southern Italian dish made with tiny waxy potatoes and the centre of the youngest artichokes. Boil both vegetables together in a little salted water. Drain well, toss in oil, lemon juice and a little crushed garlic, season to taste, chill and serve.

COEUR D'ARTICHAUT
Artichoke Bottoms

France

1

Cook 12 artichoke bottoms (3 per person) until tender with one pound (450g) of garden peas. Drain well.

2

To the hot vegetables add 3 tablespoons olive oil, several chopped tomatoes and three crushed cloves of garlic. Cook a few minutes and serve hot on a bed of red and green lettuce.

ANGINARES AVGOLEMONO
Artichokes with Egg and Lemon Sauce

Greece

Imperial (Metric)	American
6 globe artichokes	6 globe artichokes
juice of 2 lemons	juice of 2 lemons
1 onion, sliced	1 onion, sliced
3 small carrots	3 small carrots
2 oz (55g) butter	$\frac{1}{4}$ cup butter
3 crushed cloves garlic	3 crushed cloves garlic
$\frac{1}{2}$ pint (285ml) water	$1\frac{1}{3}$ cups water
2 tablespoons chopped dill	2 tablespoons chopped dill
sea salt and black pepper	sea salt and black pepper
3 egg yolks	3 egg yolks
4–5 chopped spring onions	4 to 5 chopped scallions

1
Prepare the artichokes as in the preceding recipes. Chop the onion and carrots.

2
Melt the butter in a saucepan and add the onion and garlic, cook for a few minutes then add the water and the remaining lemon juice. Throw in the carrots and artichoke bottoms with the chopped dill and seasoning. Cook for about 30 minutes. Take the pan away from the heat and let it cool a little.

3
Add the egg yolks and stir into the sauce, place back on the heat and let the sauce thicken a little. Stir in the chopped spring onions (scallions) and let the dish cool.

ANGINARES ME KOUKIA
Artichokes with Fresh Broad Beans

Greece

Imperial (Metric)	American
6 globe artichokes	6 globe artichokes
juice of 2 lemons	juice of 2 lemons
2 lb (900g) fresh broad beans	2 pounds fresh fava beans
1 large onion	1 large onion
5 fl oz (150ml) olive oil	⅔ cup olive oil
5 crushed cloves garlic	5 crushed cloves garlic
¾ pint (425ml) water	2 cups water
2 tablespoons dill	2 tablespoons dill
sea salt and black pepper	sea salt and black pepper

1

Prepare the artichokes as in the preceding recipe. Shell the broad beans and slice the onion.

2

Heat the oil in a pan and cook the onion and garlic a few minutes, add the rest of the ingredients and simmer 45 minutes.

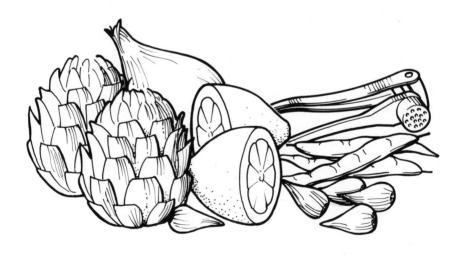

OEUFS EN GELÉES À L'ESTRAGON
Jellied Eggs with Tarragon

France

It is difficult to give precise amounts for this hors d'oeuvre but allow 1 egg per person. The eggs must be cooked *mollet*, that is, for large eggs, boiled no longer than 5 minutes so that the yolks remain runny while the white is set. The jelly is made from agar-agar which must be boiled if it is to set. Allow 2 level teaspoons per pint (570ml) of stock.

Imperial (Metric)	American
Eggs mollet (see text)	Eggs mollet (see text)
1 pint (570ml) strong vegetable stock	2½ cups strong vegetable stock
2 teaspoons agar-agar	2 teaspoons agar-agar
handful freshly chopped tarragon	handful freshly chopped tarragon
sea salt and black pepper	sea salt and black pepper

1
Carefully shell the eggs and place them in individual ramekin dishes.

2
Add to the vegetable stock the agar-agar and the chopped tarragon, boil 2–3 minutes, then let cool. While still warm and before it has set, pour it over the eggs so they are just covered.

3
Chill the dishes and allow them to set. Before serving decorate with more chopped tarragon.

OEUFS DURS EN TAPENADE

France

Another dish using eggs mollet and the tapenade purée (see page 26). Place shelled eggs into ramekin dishes, cover with a spoonful of tapenade and garnish with a little chopped hard-boiled egg.

OEUFS DURS EN AIOLI
Hard-boiled Eggs with Aioli Sauce

France

Make a thick mayonnaise with 2 egg yolks, a teaspoon of mustard, 2 crushed cloves of garlic and 10 oz (275ml or 1⅓ cups) olive oil. Boil the eggs *mollet*, place them in their ramekin dishes with a spoonful of the garlic mayonnaise and decorate with chopped parsley.

Because of their growth in Israel avocados have now become common in Mediterranean cooking. Sometimes the avocados are stuffed with a purée of cheese, onion, capers or olives; other times the flesh is extracted from the fruit and puréed with other ingredients; the flesh can also be sliced and used as a salad with other fruits and vegetables. Here is a variety of dishes common to the Middle East, France, Italy and Spain.

AVOCADO PURÉE I

France

Imperial (Metric)	American
2 avocados	2 avocados
2 crushed cloves garlic	2 crushed cloves garlic
2 tablespoons lemon juice	2 tablespoons lemon juice
5 fl oz (150ml) olive oil	⅔ cup olive oil
seasoning	seasoning

Extract flesh from avocados, place in blender with the rest of the ingredients and blend to a thick cream. Alternatively, the same amount of yogurt can be used instead of the olive oil.

PURÉ D'AGUACATE
Avocado Purée II

Spain

Imperial (Metric)	American
2 avocados	2 avocados
2 crushed cloves garlic	2 crushed cloves garlic
2 tablespoons lemon juice	2 tablespoons lemon juice
¼ pint (150ml) olive oil	⅔ cup olive oil
4 oz (100g) soft curd or cream cheese	½ cup cottage or cream cheese
bunch of spring onions, finely chopped	bunch of scallions, finely chopped
seasoning	seasoning

Take the flesh from the avocados, add the rest of the ingredients and mash them together.

INSALATA DI POMODORI, MOZZARELLA E AVOCATO
Avocado, Tomato and Mozzarella Salad

Italy

Imperial (Metric)	American
2 avocados	2 avocados
4 tomatoes	4 tomatoes
1 Italian Mozzarella cheese	1 Italian Mozzarella cheese
2 tablespoons capers	2 tablespoons capers
2 tablespoons sauce vinaigrette	2 tablespoons sauce vinaigrette

1
Stone (pit) and peel the avocados, slice the flesh, slice the tomatoes and the mozzarella cheese.

2
Arrange on a platter in alternate layers.

3
Mix the capers with the sauce vinaigrette and pour over the top.

AVOCADO AND SPINACH SALAD

France

Imperial (Metric)	American
1 lb (450g) young spinach leaves	2 cups young spinach leaves
2 avocados	2 avocados
2 crushed cloves garlic	2 crushed cloves garlic
juice of 1 lemon	juice of 1 lemon
2 tablespoons sauce vinaigrette	2 tablespoons sauce vinaigrette

1

Wash the spinach leaves and tear them from their stalks, pat dry and place in a large bowl.

2

Take the flesh from the avocados and pile it in the centre of the bowl.

3

Mix garlic, lemon juice and sauce vinaigrette and pour over the avocado.

AVOCADO SALAD

Israel

Imperial (Metric)	American
2 avocados	2 avocados
2 tomatoes	2 tomatoes
½ cucumber	½ cucumber
2 hard-boiled eggs	2 hard-cooked eggs
1 teaspoon ground coriander	1 teaspoon ground coriander
3 tablespoons sauce vinaigrette	3 tablespoons sauce vinaigrette

1

Extract the flesh from the avocados and place in a bowl.

2

Slice tomatoes, cucumber and eggs thinly, mix in with the avocado.

3

Add the coriander to the vinaigrette, pour over the salad and toss well.

ORANGE AND AVOCADO SALAD

Egypt

Imperial (Metric)	American
2 sweet oranges	2 sweet oranges
2 onions	2 onions
2 avocados	2 avocados
6 or 8 black olives, stoned and halved	6 or 8 black olives, pitted and halved
2 tablespoons sauce vinaigrette	2 tablespoons sauce vinaigrette

1

Peel the oranges, making sure all the pith is removed, and slice them with the onions.

2

Extract the flesh from the avocados and mix together, adding the olives and sauce vinaigrette.

AQUACATA RELLENAS

Stuffed Avocado

Spain

Allow one half avocado per person. Mix finely chopped spring onions (scallions), capers and a little freshly made tomato purée with curd (cottage) or cream cheese. Stuff the centre cavity and sprinkle with freshly chopped herbs including parsley or chives.

ASPARAGUS

In Spain and Italy they prefer the blanched asparagus and will happily consume that as a first course even when tinned or canned. They eat it with a little sauce vinaigrette. In France they generally prefer their asparagus green, as we do, and it is more commonly eaten hot with melted butter than in any other way.

If you are living in an asparagus growing region and have the advantage of buying it cheaply there are various dishes you can make:

Toss the cooked asparagus spears in an omelette mixture with cream. When cool, cut the omelette into pieces and enjoy it as a mezzé.

The same asparagus spears can be heated in a sauce made from cream and parmesan cheese.

Cooked asparagus can be blended into a purée and mixed with butter and cream cheese then chilled and used as a spread on hot toast.

MUSHROOM SALAD

Greece

Imperial (Metric)	American
1 lb (450g) mushrooms	8 cups mushrooms
2 tablespoons olive oil	2 tablespoons olive oil
2 teaspoons crushed coriander seeds	2 teaspoons crushed coriander seeds
2 bay leaves	2 bay leaves
salt and black pepper	salt and black pepper
juice of 1 lemon	juice of 1 lemon

Wash and slice the mushrooms. Heat the olive oil in a pan and cook the coriander seeds and bay leaves a moment to release the flavours. Add the mushrooms and seasoning. Let them cook slowly about 10 minutes, covered, then pour them with their juices into a dish. Pour the lemon juice over them.

LECHUGAS RELLENAS
Stuffed Lettuce

Spain

1

Choose a lettuce with a good heart, discard the rough outer leaves and cut out the central heart leaving enough of the heart to retain the stuffing.

2

Thinly slice 4 oz (100g or 2 cups) mushrooms and leave them an hour or two in a marinade of olive oil and wine vinegar.

3

Make a mayonnaise from egg yolks, mustard and olive oil.

4

Drain the mushrooms, mix in a tablespoon of green peppercorns and 2 or 3 tablespoons of the mayonnaise.

5

Fill the centre of the lettuce with the stuffing, chill and serve.

POMODORI RIPIENI DI RISO
Tomatoes Stuffed with Rice

Italy

Imperial (Metric)	American
6 large tomatoes	6 large tomatoes
4 tablespoons patna rice	4 tablespoons patna rice
4 tablespoons olive oil	4 tablespoons olive oil
3 garlic cloves, chopped	3 garlic cloves, chopped
2 teaspoons oregano	2 teaspoons oregano
1 tablespoon each chopped basil and parsley	1 tablespoon each chopped basil and parsley
sea salt and black pepper	sea salt and black pepper

1
Slice the top from the tomatoes and scoop out the insides. Place these, with the tops, in a blender and reduce to a purée.

2
Pour the purée into a bowl and add the rest of the ingredients reserving half the oil.

3
Oil a baking dish. Fill the tomatoes with the mixture and place them in the dish. Dribble the rest of the oil over the tomatoes and bake in a 400°F/200°C (Gas Mark 6) oven 45 minutes.

FUNGHI ALLA PALERMITANA
Palermo Baked Mushrooms

Sicily

Imperial (Metric)	American
1 lb (450g) mushrooms, cleaned	1 pound mushrooms, cleaned
5 tablespoons olive oil	5 tablespoons olive oil
3 crushed garlic cloves	3 crushed garlic cloves
1 fresh green chilli pepper, chopped	1 fresh green chili pepper, chopped
2 tablespoons parsley, chopped	2 tablespoons parsley, chopped
2 teaspoons lemon juice	2 teaspoons lemon juice
sea salt and black pepper	sea salt and black pepper
3 tablespoons wholemeal breadcrumbs	3 tablespoons whole wheat breadcrumbs
1 oz (30g) butter	2½ tablespoons butter

1

Place all ingredients in a bowl except the breadcrumbs and the butter. Mix well and let stand ½ hour.

2

Butter 6 ramekin dishes, pour equal amounts of the mushroom mixture into each one and sprinkle the top with the breadcrumbs. Place a little butter on each ramekin and bake in a 400°F/200°C (Gas Mark 6) oven 15 minutes.

UOVA SODE ALLA PUGLIESE
Hard-boiled Eggs Puglia-style

Italy

Imperial (Metric)	American
3 tablespoons olive oil	3 tablespoons olive oil
1 tablespoon red wine vinegar	1 tablespoon red wine vinegar
1 fresh green chilli, seeded and chopped	1 fresh green chili, seeded and chopped
2 tablespoons chopped fresh parsley	2 tablespoons chopped fresh parsley
2 tablespoons chopped fresh mint	2 tablespoons chopped fresh mint
3 crushed garlic cloves	3 crushed garlic cloves
4 tablespoons wholemeal breadcrumbs	4 tablespoons whole wheat breadcrumbs
sea salt	sea salt
6 hard-boiled eggs	6 hard-cooked eggs

1
Pour the oil and vinegar into a pan and cook the chilli, parsley, mint and garlic for a moment. Add the breadcrumbs and continue to cook about 3 minutes, stirring all the time; add a little salt to taste.

2
Peel the eggs and slice them in half. Pile on each one 2 teaspoons of the mixture.

VERDURE FRITTE
Fried Vegetables

Italy

Imperial (Metric)	American
Selection of cut vegetables, such as courgettes cut into chunks, fennel and tomatoes cut into wedges, mushroom caps, cauliflower florets, aubergine slices	Selection of fresh vegetables, such as zucchini cut into chunks, fennel and tomatoes cut into wedges, mushroom caps, cauliflower florets, eggplant slices
2 eggs, beaten	2 eggs, beaten
pinch of salt and black pepper	pinch of salt and black pepper
½ lb (225g) wholemeal breadcrumbs	4 cups fresh whole wheat breadcrumbs

1

Parboil cauliflower florets, fennel and courgettes (zucchini) about 2 minutes. Drain well and chill.

2

Beat the eggs and salt together in a bowl and put the breadcrumbs in another. Dip each piece of vegetable into the egg and then the breadcrumbs.

3

Fry for a few moments in olive oil so that the exterior is crisp and brown.

VEGETABLE FRITTERS

Greece

Imperial (Metric)	American
Selection of vegetables as in preceding recipe	Selection of vegetables as in preceding recipe
4 oz (100g) wholemeal flour	1 cup whole wheat flour
1 teaspoon baking powder	1 teaspoon baking powder
1 egg	1 egg
1 tablespoon olive oil	1 tablespoon olive oil
5 fl oz (150ml) water	$\frac{2}{3}$ cup water
1 tablespoon ouzo	1 tablespoon ouzo
$\frac{1}{4}$ teaspoon each powdered bay leaf, oregano and thyme	$\frac{1}{2}$ teaspoon each powdered bay leaf, oregano and thyme
sea salt and black pepper	sea salt and black pepper

1

Beat all ingredients in a mixing bowl. Let stand 1 hour then beat again before use.

2

Place the prepared vegetables, some of which need parboiling (see preceding recipe) in the batter so that they are completely coated. Fry them in deep olive oil until crisp.

Chapter 3
Salads

Salads are automatically eaten at least once a day in Mediterranean countries. It is for the most part the natural way, at least in the spring and summer, to make them with vegetables. But the salads cover a wide range from the Greek salad of Feta, black olives, tomato and perhaps lettuce, which is *de rigueur* with every meal to the lovely, lemony grain salad tabbouleh of Turkey and North Africa. In these countries yogurt is much used as a dressing while farther north, in southern France, it is supplanted by the emulsion of egg yolks and olive oil that we know as mayonnaise. Often the salads are cooked vegetables such as broad beans and cauliflower tossed warm in olive oil with freshly chopped herbs. When lettuce is used it is generally just as a basis with other leaf vegetables as in the Salade Mesclun of France or the Venetian winter salad of northern Italy. Peppers are much used, raw and thinly sliced, or sometimes with their outer skins charred and peeled away then sliced and tossed in oil and thirdly cooked as in the Turkish Pilaki. One of the most delightful experiences of eating in the Mediterranean countries is to be seated at the most modest *taverna* in the sun sipping a drink when the Patron will bring, unasked, a plate of fresh vegetables sliced and arranged with a quarter of lemon and a dribble of olive oil over them. What simplicity — but what bounty!

TABBOULEH
Bulgur Wheat Salad

Turkey

This salad from the Middle East has justly become very popular in recent years.

Imperial (Metric)	American
½ lb (225g) fine bulgur wheat	1 cup fine bulgur wheat
2 bunches spring onions	2 bunches scallions
generous handful of chopped parsley	generous handful of chopped parsley
4 fl oz (100ml) lemon juice	½ cup lemon juice
4 fl oz (100ml) olive oil	½ cup olive oil
sea salt and black pepper	sea salt and black pepper
3 crushed cloves garlic	3 crushed cloves garlic

1

Pour cold water over the bulgur wheat to about 1 inch over the surface and leave 1 hour.

2

Squeeze out any excess water and chop the spring onions (scallions) finely.

3

Add all the ingredients to the bulgur wheat and stir.

4

Serve on fresh lettuce leaves.

MOROCCAN CARROT SALAD

Morocco

Imperial (Metric)	American
3 crushed cloves garlic	3 crushed cloves garlic
$\frac{1}{2}$ teaspoon ground cumin	$\frac{1}{2}$ teaspoon ground cumin
$\frac{1}{2}$ teaspoon ground coriander	$\frac{1}{2}$ teaspoon ground coriander
2 tablespoons lemon juice	2 tablespoons lemon juice
4 tablespoons olive oil	$\frac{1}{4}$ cup olive oil
$\frac{1}{2}$ teaspoon Tabasco	$\frac{1}{2}$ teaspoon Tabasco
sea salt and black pepper	sea salt and black pepper
2 sliced red peppers	2 sliced red peppers
1 lb (450g) young cooked carrots	1 pound young cooked carrots

1

Mix the garlic and spices with the lemon juice, oil and Tabasco; add the sea salt and black pepper.

2

Cook the red peppers over a flame, blistering the skin. Turn them round slowly on a fork to ensure all the sides are done. Slice off the end and deseed them. Now slice the peppers thinly.

3

Slice the young carrots lengthways. Arrange on a platter with the red peppers and add dressing.

SALATA MI TOMATA
Tomato Salad

Greece

Imperial (Metric)	American
1 lb (450g) firm tomatoes	1 pound firm tomatoes
2 onions	2 onions
handful of fresh basil	handful of fresh basil
sauce vinaigrette	sauce vinaigrette

1

Slice the tomatoes thinly. Peel and slice the onions thinly. Lay in a shallow bowl in alternate layers.

2

Chop the fresh basil, cover the tomatoes and onions and then add the dressing.

ENSALADA DE PIMIENTO MEZCLADO
Green, Yellow and Red Pepper Salad

Spain

Imperial (Metric)	American
2 red peppers	2 red peppers
2 yellow peppers	2 yellow peppers
2 green peppers	2 green peppers
2 crushed cloves garlic	2 crushed cloves garlic
2 tablespoons lemon juice	2 tablespoons lemon juice
4 tablespoons olive oil	$\frac{1}{4}$ cup olive oil
1 teaspoon ground cumin	1 teaspoon ground cumin
$\frac{1}{2}$ teaspoon Tabasco	$\frac{1}{2}$ teaspoon Tabasco
sea salt and black pepper	sea salt and black pepper

1
Blister the skins of the peppers over a flame as described under Moroccan Carrot Salad (page 52).

2
Cut the stalks away and discard the seeds. Slice the peppers thinly. Arrange on a dish in coloured stripes.

3
Mix the rest of the ingredients and pour this dressing over the peppers. Chill and serve.

Note:
There is a new variety of black pepper now becoming available. Use this in the salad as well.

POMMES DE TERRE À LA MAYONNAISE
Potato Salad

France

Imperial (Metric)	American
2 tablespoons olive oil	2 tablespoons olive oil
1 tablespoon lemon juice	1 tablespoon lemon juice
1 lb (450g) new waxy potatoes	1 pound new waxy potatoes
bunch of spring onions or chives	bunch of scallions or chives
1 teaspoon moutarde de Meaux	1 teaspoon moutarde de Meaux
2 egg yolks	2 egg yolks
8 fl oz (225ml) olive oil	1 cup olive oil
8 fl oz (225ml) yogurt	1 cup yogurt
sea salt and black pepper	sea salt and black pepper

1
In a large bowl mix the olive oil and lemon juice with a little salt and pepper.

2
Boil the potatoes in their skins until tender. Drain them well. While still hot, cut them into quarters and add them to the oil and lemon juice.

3
Chop the spring onions (scallions) or chives and add to the potatoes.

4
Make a mayonnaise by stirring the mustard into the egg yolks and adding the olive oil, drop by drop. Season to taste — it may need a little crushed garlic. Beat in the yogurt.

5
Add enough of this yogurt mayonnaise to the potato salad to make it into a rich feast. Excellent served on crisp cos lettuce.

SALADE PROVENÇALE

One of the most famous salads in the world is Salad Niçoise, which is a hybrid mixture of lettuce, black olives, cucumber, anchovies, tuna fish and hard-boiled egg. This salad stems from Provence and there are many versions. Sometimes, for a luncheon dish, a round loaf is half hollowed out, the salad placed in the cavity, a weight placed on the loaf and the whole chilled overnight. The loaf is then cut like a cake. This could be done with the following salad, too, which is a vegetarian version of these Provençale salads.

Imperial (Metric)	American
1 crisp lettuce	1 crisp lettuce
½ cucumber	½ cucumber
4 tomatoes	4 tomatoes
bunch spring onions	bunch scallions
3 hard-boiled eggs	3 hard-cooked eggs
4 oz (100g) bean curd (tofu)	½ cup tofu
vegetable oil for sautéing	vegetable oil for sautéing
2 tablespoons soy sauce	2 tablespoons soy sauce
3 crushed cloves garlic	3 crushed cloves garlic
1 tablespoon lemon juice	1 tablespoon lemon juice
3 tablespoons olive oil	3 tablespoons olive oil
4oz (100g) cooked haricot beans	⅔ cup cooked navy beans
salt and black pepper	salt and black pepper
12 black olives, stoned and halved	12 black olives, pitted and halved
2 tablespoons capers	2 tablespoons capers

1
Break up the lettuce leaves and place in a large bowl.

2
Slice cucumber, tomatoes and spring onions (scallions) and scatter over the lettuce with the olives. Quarter the hard-boiled eggs and add.

3

Slice the bean curd (tofu) and sauté in the vegetable oil until crisp. Pour the soy sauce into the pan, raise the heat and let the bean curd (tofu) absorb it.

4

Add garlic, lemon juice and olive oil to the beans. Season and sprinkle with olives & capers. Scatter the tofu pieces over the salad and pour the bean sauce over it all.

SALADE DES GROS FÈVES
Broad Bean Salad

France

Imperial (Metric)	American
1 lb fresh young broad beans	2½ cups fresh young fava beans
3 tablespoons olive oil	3 tablespoons olive oil
1 tablespoon lemon juice	1 tablespoon lemon juice
sea salt and black pepper	sea salt and black pepper
1 crushed clove garlic	1 crushed clove garlic
handful chopped mint and parsley	handful chopped mint and parsley

1

Shell the beans and boil them until just done.

2

Mix the dressing with the garlic. Drain the beans and while they are still hot toss them in the dressing with the herbs.

SPINACH YOGURT SALAD

Egypt

Imperial (Metric)	American
1 lb (450g) young fresh spinach	2 cups young fresh spinach
1 crushed clove garlic	1 crushed clove garlic
1 tablespoon pickled green peppercorns	1 tablespoon pickled green peppercorns
sea salt	sea salt
5 fl oz (150ml) yogurt	$\frac{2}{3}$ cup yogurt

1

Tear the stalks from the spinach; place leaves in a saucepan and cook 1–2 minutes, stirring all the time, so that the leaves are neither raw nor quite cooked. Take away from the heat.

2

Mix the garlic, green peppercorns and sea salt into the yogurt.

3

Place the spinach leaves in a bowl and pour the dressing over them, toss well and serve.

RAW BEETROOT (BEET) SALAD

Malta

Imperial (Metric)	American
$\frac{1}{2}$ lb (225g) beetroot	$\frac{1}{2}$ pound beets
2 tablespoons olive oil	2 tablespoons olive oil
2 tablespoons lemon juice	2 tablespoons lemon juice
5 fl oz (150ml) yogurt	$\frac{2}{3}$ cup yogurt
sea salt and black pepper	sea salt and black pepper

1
Peel and grate the beetroot (beets) into a bowl.

2
Mix the rest of the ingredients and pour over the beetroot (beets), stir well and serve.

INSALATE DI ZUCCHINNI PICCOLO
Baby Courgette or Zucchini Salad

Italy

1
Pick the courgettes (zucchini) so young that they still have their flowers on. Allow 3 per person. Slice each courgette (zucchini) 4 times, but do not cut through to the head, where the flower is. They should resemble an old-fashioned clothes peg with four legs).

2
Steam these very briefly (2 to 3 minutes). Use the dressing for the broad bean salad, pour it over the courgettes (zucchini), chill and serve.

PIAZ

Turkey

Imperial (Metric)	American
½ lb (225g) cooked haricot beans	1 cup cooked navy beans
6 black olives, stoned and halved	6 black olives, pitted and halved
2 hard-boiled eggs	2 hard-cooked eggs
2 tomatoes	2 tomatoes
3 crushed cloves garlic	3 crushed cloves garlic
1 tablespoon lemon juice	1 tablespoon lemon juice
3 tablespoons olive oil	3 tablespoons olive oil
sea salt and black pepper	sea salt and black pepper

1
Place the cooked beans in a bowl and add the olives.

2
Slice the eggs and tomatoes and add. Mix the garlic, lemon juice and olive oil, pour over the beans and stir well.

3
Leave a few hours for the beans to absorb the flavour.

GREEK SALAD

Greece

Imperial (Metric)	American
1 lb (450g) tomatoes	1 pound tomatoes
½ cucumber	½ cucumber
6 oz (170g) Feta cheese	¾ cup Feta cheese
10 black olives stoned and halved	10 black olives pitted and halved
3 tablespoons olive oil	3 tablespoons olive oil
1 teaspoon wine vinegar	1 teaspoon wine vinegar
sea salt and black pepper	sea salt and black pepper
2 tablespoons chopped marjoram	2 tablespoons chopped marjoram

1
Chop the tomatoes into quarters, slice the cucumber into chunks and cube the cheese.

2
Place these in a bowl with the rest of the ingredients and stir well.

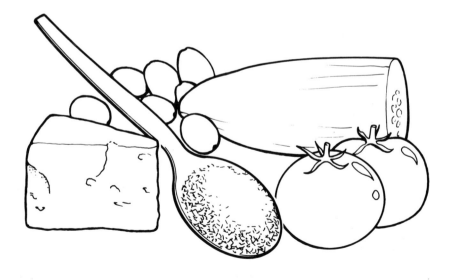

POMODORO, FINOCCHIO E MOZZARELLA
Tomato, Fennel and Mozzarella

Italy

Imperial (Metric)	American
1 lb (450g) tomatoes	1 pound tomatoes
2 heads fennel	2 heads fennel
2 Italian Mozzarella cheeses	2 Italian Mozzarella cheeses
3 tablespoons finely chopped basil	$\frac{1}{4}$ cup finely chopped basil
3 tablespoons olive oil	3 tablespoons olive oil
1 tablespoon red wine vinegar	1 tablespoon red wine vinegar
sea salt and black pepper	sea salt and black pepper

1

Slice the tomatoes, fennel and Mozzarella. Lay on a platter in alternate layers.

2

Scatter the basil leaves over the dish. Mix the dressing and pour over everything. Chill and serve.

PILAKI

Turkey

Imperial (Metric)	American
2 green peppers	2 green peppers
2 red peppers	2 red peppers
2 yellow peppers	2 yellow peppers
3 large onions	3 large onions
4 tomatoes	4 tomatoes
15–20 whole garlic cloves	15–20 whole garlic cloves
6 fl oz (175ml) olive oil	$\frac{3}{4}$ cup olive oil
1 teaspoon cumin seeds	1 teaspoon cumin seeds
1 teaspoon oregano	1 teaspoon oregano
$\frac{1}{2}$ teaspoon crushed coriander	$\frac{1}{2}$ teaspoon crushed coriander
$\frac{1}{2}$ teaspoon Tabasco	$\frac{1}{2}$ teaspoon Tabasco
6 fl oz (175ml) water	$\frac{3}{4}$ cup water
sea salt	sea salt

1

Seed, core and cut the peppers into strips, quarter the onions, halve the tomatoes and peel the garlic cloves.

2

Heat the oil in a large pan and add the spices, then all the vegetables. Stir them in the oil about 4 minutes.

3

Add the Tabasco to the water, then add the water slowly to the oil, sprinkle with a little salt, lower the heat and let the vegetables simmer until soft — about 15 minutes. This is eaten cold and is best if left 24 hours.

CHICKPEA (GARBANZO) SALAD

Egypt

Imperial (Metric)	American
1 lb (450g) dried chickpeas	2 cups dried garbanzos
2 raw carrots	2 raw carrots
2 raw beetroot	2 raw beets
2 raw turnips	2 raw turnips
5 tablespoons olive oil	$\frac{1}{3}$ cup olive oil
1 teaspoon curry powder	1 teaspoon curry powder
1 teaspoon garam masala	1 teaspoon garam masala
sea salt and black pepper	sea salt and black pepper
2 tablespoons lemon juice with zest	2 tablespoons lemon juice with zest
1 tablespoon honey	1 tablespoon honey

1

Soak the chickpeas (garbanzos) overnight. Boil them in plenty of water for 2 hours or until tender. Drain well.

2

Grate the vegetables and mix with the chickpeas (garbanzos).

3

Heat the olive oil, add the curry powder and garam masala and let the spices cook in the oil a few minutes, stirring well. Allow to cool and add the lemon juice, zest, honey, salt and pepper.

3

Pour over the salad and let it soak at least 2 hours, but no harm will be done if left for a day.

FUL SALAD
Egyptian Brown Bean Salad

Egypt

Imperial (Metric)	American
½ lb (225g) ful beans	1¼ cup ful beans
1 bunch spring onions	1 bunch scallions
3 tablespoons capers	3 tablespoons capers
generous handful chopped fresh mint	generous handful chopped fresh mint
generous handful chopped fresh parsley	generous handful chopped fresh parsley
5 crushed cloves garlic	5 crushed cloves garlic
½ teaspoon sea salt	½ teaspoon sea salt
freshly ground black pepper	freshly ground black pepper
juice and zest of 1 lemon	juice and zest of 1 lemon
3 fl oz (90ml) olive oil	⅓ cup olive oil

1
Soak the ful beans overnight and boil them in plenty of water until tender. Drain them.

2
Place the beans in a large bowl, chop the spring onions (scallions) and add them with the rest of the ingredients to the beans.

3
Stir thoroughly and leave a few hours before serving.

LENTIL SALAD

Turkey

Imperial (Metric)	American
¾ lb (350g) green lentils	2 cups green lentils
6 shallots	6 shallots
2 bay leaves	2 bay leaves
juice and peel of 1 lemon	juice and peel of 1 lemon
3 tablespoons olive oil	3 tablespoons olive oil
½ teaspoon ground cumin	½ teaspoon ground cumin
½ teaspoon ground coriander	½ teaspoon ground coriander
sea salt and black pepper	sea salt and black pepper

1
Soak the lentils in cold water for 1 hour. Peel and quarter the shallots and add to the lentils with the lemon peel and bay leaves.

2
Boil the lentils for 30 minutes or until tender. They should not disintegrate into a purée.

3
Drain lentils, discard the lemon peel and bay leaves and add the olive oil, lemon juice, spices and seasoning. Garnish with sprigs of parsley and a little chopped mint.

SALATA ME FASOLYA PRASINA
Green Bean Salad

Greece

Imperial (Metric)	American
1 lb (450g) green beans	1 pound green beans
4–5 shallots	4–5 shallots
3 tomatoes	3 tomatoes
juice and zest of 1 lemon	juice and zest of 1 lemon
3 fl oz (90ml) olive oil	$\frac{1}{3}$ cup olive oil
sea salt and black pepper	sea salt and black pepper
generous handful chopped	generous handful chopped
parsley	parsley

1
Trim and cut the beans into 2-inch (5cm) pieces. Boil them in a little salted water until just tender. Do not overcook.

2
Slice the shallots very thinly and also slice the tomatoes. Drain the beans and place them in a bowl with the shallots and tomatoes.

3
Mix the lemon juice, olive oil and seasoning. Pour over the vegetables, sprinkle with parsley and serve.

CHICKPEA (GARBANZO) AND BULGUR WHEAT SALAD

Lebanon

Imperial (Metric)	American
½ lb (225g) chickpeas	1 cup garbanzos
4 oz (100g) bulgur wheat	½ cup bulgur wheat
3 tablespoons olive oil	3 tablespoons olive oil
4 oz (100g) tomato purée	⅔ cup tomato paste
1 bunch spring onions	1 bunch scallions
juice and zest of 1 lemon	juice and zest of 1 lemon
sea salt and black pepper	sea salt and black pepper
handful of chopped parsley	handful of chopped parsley

1

Soak the chickpeas (garbanzos) overnight. Boil them in plenty of water for a good 2 hours.

2

Place the bulgur wheat in a bowl and add some of the chickpea (garbanzo) liquid so that the wheat is covered by 1 inch of water. Let it absorb the water 1 hour.

3

Drain the rest of the liquid from the chickpeas (garbanzos). Add the olive oil and tomato paste and let simmer a few minutes.

4

Chop the spring onions (scallions) and add to the bulgur wheat, then add the chickpeas (garbanzos) and their sauce. Add the lemon juice and zest, season and mix the salad well. Add the chopped parsley and serve.

HARICOT (NAVY) BEAN SALAD

Turkey

Imperial (Metric)	American
½ lb (225g) haricot beans	1¼ cups navy beans
2 eggs	2 eggs
2 onions	2 onions
2 tomatoes	2 tomatoes
12 black olives	12 black olives
juice and zest of 1 lemon	juice and zest of 1 lemon
4 tablespoons olive oil	¼ cup olive oil
sea salt and black pepper	sea salt and black pepper

1

Soak the beans overnight then boil until just tender, about 1 hour.

2

Hard-boil the eggs, shell and slice them. Thinly slice the onions and tomatoes. Stone (pit) and halve the olives.

3

Drain the beans well and add the rest of the ingredients. Stir the salad carefully so that the egg and vegetable combination does not disintegrate.

SPICED CUCUMBER

Morocco

Imperial (Metric)	American
5–6 shallots	5–6 shallots
3 chilli peppers	3 chili peppers
2 oz (55g) ginger root	2 ounces ginger root
4 tablespoons olive oil	¼ cup olive oil
1 tablespoon red wine vinegar	1 tablespoon red wine vinegar
sea salt	sea salt
1 large cucumber	1 large cucumber

1

Peel and slice the shallots and slice peppers thinly. Peel the ginger root and grate it. Add all this to the olive oil, vinegar and salt. Stir well.

2

Dice the unpeeled cucumber into ¼-inch (6mm) cubes. Add this to the oil and let marinate a few hours.

Note:
This is a hot dish and is more of a pickle than a salad.

JAJIKI
Cucumber and Yogurt Sauce

Greece

This is eaten all over the Middle East and in Greece and is particularly cool and refreshing.

1

Do not peel the cucumber. Slice it lengthways into 8 strips, then cut it across into $\frac{1}{4}$-inch (6mm) pieces. Place it in a colander and sprinkle with salt. Leave it 2 hours so that it loses much of its water, then wash the salt from it.

2

Chop a handful of fresh mint. Grind a little pepper over the cucumber and add it and the mint to as much yogurt as will make a liquid but chunky sauce.

MICHOTETA

Imperial (Metric)	American
½ lb (225g) Feta cheese	1 cup Feta cheese
juice and zest of 1 lemon	juice and zest of 1 lemon
3 tablespoons olive oil	3 tablespoons olive oil
1 cucumber	1 cucumber
2 onions	2 onions
black pepper	black pepper

1

Place the cheese in a bowl and work in the lemon juice and olive oil, mashing the cheese with a fork.

2

Dice the cucumber into cubes, slice the onion thinly and add to the cheese. Season with black pepper (if using Feta you will need no salt).

CREAM CHEESE AND CELERY SALAD

Malta

Imperial (Metric)	American
½ lb (225g) cream cheese	1 cup cream cheese
5 fl oz (150ml) yogurt	⅔ cup yogurt
juice and zest of 1 lemon	juice and zest of 1 lemon
2 tablespoons olive oil	2 tablespoons olive oil
sea salt and white pepper	sea salt and white pepper
1 head celery	1 head celery

1

Mix the cream cheese with the yogurt, lemon juice, oil, salt and pepper.

2

Chop the celery finely, add it to the cheese and yogurt, stir well and serve.

72

TOURETO

Israel

Imperial (Metric)	American
6 slices wholemeal bread	6 slices whole wheat bread
1 large cucumber	1 large cucumber
3 crushed cloves garlic	3 crushed cloves garlic
3 tablespoons olive oil	3 tablespoons olive oil
juice and zest of 1 lemon	juice and zest of 1 lemon
1 teaspoon paprika	1 teaspoon paprika
sea salt and black pepper	sea salt and black pepper

1
Soak the bread in water 1 hour. Squeeze it dry and place in a blender.

2
Cut the cucumber into chunks and add to the bread in the blender with the rest of the ingredients.

3
Blend until you have a purée. Serve garnished with parsley.

SALADE DE PISSENLITS
Dandelion Leaf Salad

France

Pick dandelion leaves when they are young and toss them in a simple garlic vinaigrette. Alternatively, the leaves can be mixed with different lettuces.

SALADE MESCLUN

France

This salad, composed of many tiny green leaves and sold and packaged in the markets of the south of France, starts with the thinnings from lettuce and spinach seedlings. Added to this are endive (chicory), rocket, purslane, corn salad or lambs lettuce, and dandelion. It is served in France as a first course with a garlic vinaigrette, sometimes with the addition of garlic croûtons.

SALADE ROUGE À LA LANGUEDOCIENNE

France

Imperial (Metric)	American
1 small red lettuce heart	1 small red lettuce heart
1 heart curly endive	1 heart chicory
small bunch of rocket	small bunch of rocket
1 teaspoon chopped fresh savory	1 teaspoon chopped fresh savory
3 oz (75g) Gruyère cheese, diced	1 cup Gruyère cheese diced
2 tablespoons olive oil	2 tablespoons olive oil
1 teaspoon red wine vinegar	1 teaspoon red wine vinegar
sea salt and black pepper	sea salt and black pepper

1

Scatter the leaves in a large bowl and sprinkle the savory over it.

2

Dice the Gruyère cheese into $\frac{1}{4}$-inch (6mm) cubes and scatter these over the salad.

3

Mix the oil, vinegar and seasoning together and just before serving pour over the salad and toss well.

SALADE DE RIZ

Rice Salad

France

Imperial (Metric)	American
½ lb (225g) brown rice	1 cup brown rice
1 lemon	1 lemon
1 green and 1 yellow pepper	1 green and 1 yellow pepper
4–5 tomatoes	4–5 tomatoes
2 hard-boiled eggs	2 hard-cooked eggs
2 tablespoons each chopped chives and tarragon	2 tablespoons each chopped chives and tarragon
generous grating of nutmeg	generous grating of nutmeg
4 tablespoons olive oil	4 tablespoons olive oil
1 tablespoon tarragon vinegar	1 tablespoon tarragon vinegar
sea salt and black pepper	sea salt and black pepper

1

Cover the rice generously with water. Peel the lemon and squeeze out the juice. Add juice and lemon peel with a pinch of salt to the rice. Boil until rice is tender, about 40 minutes.

2

Discard lemon peel, drain the rice and dry it out in a low oven.

3

Seed the peppers and slice them into rounds. Slice the tomatoes and the eggs.

4

Put the dry rice in a bowl, add the chives, tarragon and nutmeg. Mix the oil and tarragon vinegar with the seasoning and pour over the salad.

WINTER SALAD

Italy

If you visit Venice in the winter you will find this salad, which is based upon the red-leaved radicchio, but there are many types including dark-coloured leaf that is almost purple, a spotted green and red radicchio and a striped red, pink and green trevisio. These are often mixed together and served with vinaigrette sauce. These leaves are becoming increasingly available outside Italy but they also grow well in English and North American gardens and will turn a darker shade of red the colder it becomes.

BROAD (FAVA) BEAN SALAD WITH BASIL

Greece

Imperial (Metric)	American
1 lb (450g) fresh, shelled young broad beans	1 pound fresh, shelled, young fava beans
5 tablespoons olive oil	5 tablespoons olive oil
2 tablespoons lemon juice	2 tablespoons lemon juice
sea salt and black pepper	sea salt and black pepper
10 black olives, stoned and halved	10 black olives, pitted and halved
bunch of spring onions	bunch of scallions
3 tablespoons freshly chopped basil	3 tablespoons freshly chopped basil

1

Cook the beans in a little salted water 8 minutes or until tender. Drain well.

2

Pour the oil, lemon juice and seasoning into a mixing bowl. Add the cooked beans and the olives. Chop up the spring onions (scallions) and add.

3

Toss the salad well and sprinkle with the chopped basil.

RED SLAW

Malta

Imperial (Metric)	American
5 fl oz (150ml) olive oil	⅔ cup olive oil
2 tablespoons red wine vinegar	2 tablespoons red wine vinegar
1 tablespoon moutarde de Meaux	1 tablespoon moutarde de Meaux
3 crushed cloves garlic	3 crushed cloves garlic
sea salt and black pepper	sea salt and black pepper
1 medium-sized red cabbage	1 medium-sized red cabbage
2 cooking apples	2 cooking apples
1 head celery	1 head celery

1

In a large mixing bowl mix the oil, vinegar, mustard, garlic and seasonings to form a thick vinaigrette sauce.

2

Trim and quarter the cabbage and grate it into the vinaigrette sauce. Do the same with the apples. Toss thoroughly so that both are coated with the sauce.

3

Chop the celery and add it to the salad, mix well and serve.

SPINACH AND MUSHROOM SALAD

Malta

Imperial (Metric)	American
½ lb (225g) mushrooms	4 cups mushrooms
1 bunch spring onions	1 bunch scallions
¾ lb (340g) young spinach leaves	12 ounces young spinach leaves
2 tablespoons chopped parsley	2 tablespoons chopped parsley
5 fl oz (150ml) olive oil	⅔ cup olive oil
1 tablespoon red wine vinegar	1 tablespoon red wine vinegar
1 tablespoon lemon juice	1 tablespoon lemon juice
3 crushed cloves garlic,	3 crushed cloves garlic,
sea salt and black pepper	sea salt and black pepper

1

In a large salad bowl mix the oil, vinegar, lemon juice, garlic and seasoning. Slice the mushrooms with their stalks and add them to the vinaigrette with the chopped spring onions (scallions).

2

Tear the spinach leaves from their stalks and add the leaves to the salad; sprinkle with the chopped parsley and toss well.

CÉLERI DE CORSE
Corsican Celeriac Salad

France

Imperial (Metric)	American
1 medium-sized celeriac	1 medium-sized celeriac
6 cooked artichoke bottoms	6 cooked artichoke bottoms
½ pint (285ml) mayonnaise	1⅓ cups mayonnaise
2 tablespoons chopped parsley	2 tablespoons chopped parsley
sea salt and black pepper	sea salt and black pepper

1

Peel the celeriac and cut it into very fine julienne strips. Place in a bowl and pour boiling water over it, leave 1 minute and then drain.

2

Cut the artichoke bottoms into julienne strips and in a mixing bowl combine all the ingredients.

INSALATE DI FINOCCHIO
Fennel Salad

Imperial (Metric)	American
3 fennel roots	3 fennel roots
5 tablespoons olive oil	5 tablespoons olive oil
2 tablespoons lemon juice	2 tablespoons lemon juice
1 tablespoon chopped mint	1 tablespoon chopped mint
sea salt and black pepper	sea salt and black pepper

1

Trim the fennel roots and discard any tough outer leaves. Slice thinly across the roots.

2

Mix the rest of the ingredients in a large bowl and add the sliced fennel, mixing thoroughly.

Chapter 4
Soups

SOUPE À L'AIL
Garlic Soup

France

Imperial (Metric)	American
4 heads garlic	4 heads garlic
5 fl oz (150ml) olive oil	$\frac{2}{3}$ cup olive oil
3 egg yolks	3 egg yolks
sea salt and black pepper	sea salt and black pepper
2 pints (1.2 litres) vegetable stock	5 cups vegetable stock

1
Trim and peel the garlic cloves; if they are large, cut them into thin slices.
Pour the oil into a saucepan, put the garlic into the oil and sauté a few
minutes. Add the vegetable stock and simmer $\frac{1}{2}$ hour.

2
Let the soup cool and blend. Taste and season the soup. Reheat and stir in
the egg yolks until soup thickens a little.

There are many different versions of garlic soup in France, Italy and Spain;
here are some variations.

GARLIC SOUP WITH SAFFRON AND POTATOES

Spain

Make as for garlic soup but omit the egg yolks. After blending the garlic and its liquid return the soup to the saucepan with 3 peeled and diced potatoes and a pinch of saffron. Simmer another 20 minutes so that the potatoes are tender. Sprinkle with chopped parsley and serve.

II GARLIC SOUP WITH FRESH HERBS

France

Make this, too, as for the basic garlic soup, but add to the olive oil and the garlic cloves, $\frac{1}{4}$ teaspoon each crushed bay leaf, sage and thyme and $\frac{1}{2}$ teaspoon oregano. Simmer for the same amount of time, blend, then add the egg yolks.

III GARLIC SOUP WITH POACHED EGG

Spain

After blending the garlic soup, reheat it until just simmering. Carefully break an egg for each person into the soup and poach them in it. Toast a piece of bread for each egg, put the toast in individual soup bowls, pour the soup in and slide the poached egg on top of the toast. Garnish with chopped parsley and a little grated Parmesan.

SOUPE AU PISTOU

France

Imperial (Metric)	American
4 oz (100g) dried haricot beans soaked and drained	¾ cup dried navy beans soaked and drained
3½ pints (2 litres) water	9 cups water
3 medium carrots, diced	3 medium carrots, diced
3 medium potatoes, diced	3 medium potatoes, diced
3 medium courgettes, chopped	3 medium zucchini, chopped
2 leeks, chopped	2 leeks, chopped
1 lb (450g) tomatoes, peeled	1 pound tomatoes, peeled
4 oz (100g) green French beans, chopped	4 ounces green beans, chopped
4 oz (100g) shelled green peas	¾ cup shelled green peas
bouquet garni	bouquet garni
2½ oz (75g) small noodles	½ cup small noodles
sea salt and black pepper	sea salt and black pepper

1

Boil the dried beans in the water 1 hour, add the other vegetables and the bouquet garni and simmer another 45 minutes. You may need a little more water. Add the noodles and cook a further 10 minutes.

2

Taste and season, discard the bouquet garni. Take the soup from the heat and put into a serving dish; now add the pistou sauce (below) stirring it into the soup.

3

Serve and have a bowl of freshly grated Parmesan on the table to sprinkle over the soup.

PISTOU SAUCE

France

Imperial (Metric)	American
20 basil leaves	20 basil leaves
3 crushed cloves garlic	3 crushed cloves garlic
4 oz (100g) freshly grated Parmesan	1 cup freshly grated Parmesan
3 fl oz (90ml) olive oil	$\frac{1}{3}$ cup olive oil
sea salt and black pepper	sea salt and black pepper

In a blender pour the oil over the basil and garlic, process, shredding the leaves into a thin green purée. Add the seasoning and the cheese to make a thick sauce. Splendid also with pasta.

ZUPPA DI CAVOLO
Cabbage Soup

Italy

Imperial (Metric)	American
$\frac{1}{2}$ lb (225g) borlotti beans	1$\frac{1}{4}$ cups pinto beans
3 tablespoons olive oil	3 tablespoons olive oil
2 onions, chopped	2 onions, chopped
head of celery, chopped	head of celery, chopped
1 white cabbage, shredded	1 white cabbage, shredded
sea salt and freshly ground black pepper	sea salt and freshly ground black pepper
handful of freshly chopped basil	handful of freshly chopped basil

1
Soak the beans overnight then cook until tender, about 2 hours.

2
Heat the olive oil in another pan and add the onion, celery and cabbage. Stir, cover the pan and leave over a low flame to cook in their own juices, about 10 minutes.

3
Take out half of the beans with their liquid and blend to a thin purée, add the rest of the beans to the vegetables, then add the bean purée. Stir well.

4
Reheat and let simmer a few moments before turning off the heat and adding the chopped basil.

ZUPPA DI CANNELINI CON AGLIO
Garlic Bean Soup

Italy

Imperial (Metric)	American
1 lb (450g) haricot beans	1 pound navy beans
3 pints (1.7 litres) celery stock	7½ cups celery stock
sprig of bay leaves	sprig of bay leaves
1 head garlic	1 head garlic
4 tablespoons olive oil	¼ cup olive oil
sea salt and black pepper	sea salt and black pepper
handful fresh parsley	handful fresh parsley
1 teaspoon dried oregano	1 teaspoon dried oregano

1

Soak beans overnight then cook them in the celery stock with the bay leaves until tender, about 1½ hours. Cover the pan but check every 15 minutes that they have not absorbed all the stock. If so add water.

2

Peel all the cloves of garlic from the head, slice them and add them to the olive oil in a saucepan. Sauté them in the oil for a few minutes then, discarding the bay leaves, add the beans, season with sea salt and stir in the chopped parsley.

POTAGE CRESSONIÈRE À LA CRÈME

Cream of Watercress and Potato Soup

France

Imperial (Metric)	American
2 bunches watercress	2 bunches watercress
1½ lb (675g) potatoes	1½ pounds potatoes
3 pints (1.7 litres) water	7½ cups water
½ pint (285ml) thick cream	1⅓ cups heavy cream
2 egg yolks	2 egg yolks
sea salt and white pepper	sea salt and white pepper

1

Cut the stalks from the watercress, peel and dice the potatoes, add both to the water and boil until potatoes are cooked, about 15 minutes. Discard the watercress stalks.

2

Place the potatoes and their liquid in a blender, add the watercress leaves, cream and egg yolks. Blend until leaves are green purée . Season with salt and pepper. Reheat with care — do not allow it to boil.

GAZPACHO

Imperial (Metric)	American
1 lb (450g) tomatoes	1 pound tomatoes
2 onions, chopped	2 onions, chopped
2 peppers	2 peppers
2 crushed cloves garlic	2 crushed cloves garlic
2 tablespoons wine vinegar	2 tablespoons wine vinegar
1 teaspoon paprika	1 teaspoon paprika
sea salt and black pepper	sea salt and black pepper
1 cucumber, chopped	1 cucumber, chopped

1

Place the tomatoes in a blender and process until they disintegrate in their own liquid. Add the onion to the blender and repeat. Core and deseed the peppers and add them to the blender with the garlic cloves. Add the vinegar, paprika and seasoning.

2

Pour everything into a bowl and chill at least 2 hours.

3

Put the cucumber in the blender and reduce to a liquid. Add to the soup and before serving add several ice cubes.

GAZPACHO MARINA

Spain

Imperial (Metric)	American
1 lb (450g) tomatoes	1 pound tomatoes
2 onions	2 onions
2 oz (55g) peeled blanched almonds	½ cup peeled blanched almonds
3 slices wholemeal bread	3 slices whole wheat bread
5 fl oz (150ml) olive oil	⅔ cup olive oil
2 tablespoons red wine vinegar	2 tablespoons red wine vinegar
1 cucumber	1 cucumber
sea salt and black pepper	sea salt and black pepper

1

Blend tomatoes, onions and cucumber as in the preceding recipe. Pour into a bowl.

2

Put the almonds and olive oil in the blender and process until almonds are crushed. Add about a cup of water, the vinegar and the seasoning with the slices of bread. Blend until they are disintegrated; add this to the soup. Taste for seasoning.

3

Chill well before serving.

SOPA DE CREMA DE SETAS
Cream of Mushroom Soup

Spain

Imperial (Metric)	American
½ lb (225g) mushrooms	4 cups mushrooms
1 onion	1 onion
3 tablespoons olive oil	3 tablespoons olive oil
3 oz (85g) fresh brown breadcrumbs	1½ cups fresh brown breadcrumbs
2 pints (1.2 litres) vegetable stock	5 cups vegetable stock
2 egg yolks	2 egg yolks
¼ pint (150ml) thick cream	⅔ cup heavy cream
sea salt and black pepper	sea salt and black pepper

1
Slice the mushrooms and onion, heat the oil in a pan and cook the mushrooms, onions and breadcrumbs a few minutes.

2
Add the vegetable stock and simmer ¼ hour.

3
Blend the soup to a thin purée. Mix the yolks with the cream. Pour the soup back into the pan, add the cream and reheat carefully. Do not let boil. Serve with garlic croûtons and a little chopped parsley.

POTAGE CRÉCY
Carrot Soup

France

Imperial (Metric)	American
1 lb (450g) young carrots	1 pound young carrots
3–4 shallots	3–4 shallots
2 oz (55g) butter	$\frac{1}{4}$ cup butter
2 pints (1.2 litres) vegetable stock	5 cups vegetable stock
pinch nutmeg	pinch nutmeg
2 tablespoons thick cream	2 tablespoons heavy cream
sea salt and black pepper	sea salt and black pepper

1

Slice the carrots and shallots, melt butter in saucepan and cook the
vegetables a few minutes. Add stock and nutmeg.

2

Simmer 20 minutes. Let the soup cool, then blend, adding the cream and
seasoning. Reheat with care. Do not let the soup boil or the cream will
curdle.

CRÈME TOULOUSOISE
Cream of Onion and Potato Soup

France

Imperial (Metric)	American
¼ lb (225g) potatoes	½ pound potatoes
½ lb (225g) onions	½ pound onions
2 large leeks	2 large leeks
2 oz (55g) butter	¼ cup butter
2 pints (1.2 litres) vegetable stock	5 cups vegetable stock
5 fl oz (150ml) single cream	⅔ cup light cream
sea salt and black pepper	sea salt and black pepper
handful of chopped parsley	handful of chopped parsley

1
Slice all the vegetables and cook them in the butter a few minutes. Add the vegetable stock and simmer 20 minutes.

2
Let soup cool then blend; add the cream. Check seasoning.

3
Reheat with care, stirring in the parsley at the last moment.

PURÉE LEONTINE

France

Imperial (Metric)	American
2 lb (900g) leeks	2 pounds leeks
4 oz (100g) spinach	$\frac{1}{2}$ cup spinach
1 lettuce	1 lettuce
4 oz (100g) fresh green peas, (shelled)	$\frac{3}{4}$ cup fresh green peas (shelled)
5 fl oz (150ml) olive oil	$\frac{2}{3}$ cup olive oil
juice of 2 lemons	juice of 2 lemons
2 pints (1.2 litres) vegetable stock	5 cups vegetable stock
sea salt and black pepper	sea salt and black pepper
2 tablespoons each chopped parsley and mint	2 tablespoons each chopped parsley and mint

1
Heat the olive oil in a saucepan. Slice the leeks, spinach and lettuce. Add them with the peas to the oil. Place over low heat and simmer 10 minutes.

2
Add the lemon juice and vegetable stock, cook another 10 minutes. Let the soup cool then blend.

3
Add the seasoning and stir in the herbs before reheating.

BEID BI LAMOUN

Egg and Lemon Soup

Egypt

Imperial (Metric)	American
3 pints (1.7 litres) celery stock	7½ cups celery stock
2 oz (50g) rice	¼ cup rice
juice of 3 lemons with zest	juice of 3 lemons with zest
3 egg yolks	3 egg yolks
sea salt and black pepper	sea salt and black pepper
3 tablespoons chopped parsley	3 tablespoons chopped parsley

1

Heat the stock and add the rice and lemon zest and let simmer until rice is done.

2

Add the lemon juice to the stock. Place the egg yolks in a bowl and add a little of the stock to them. Stir well. Add to the soup, stirring all the time until soup just thickens.

3

Taste and adjust the seasoning. Add the herbs before serving.

LENTIL SOUP

Turkey

Imperial (Metric)	American
2 oz (55g) butter	¼ cup butter
½ lb (225g) orange lentils	1 cup orange lentils
1 chopped onion	1 chopped onion
1 teaspoon ground cumin	1 teaspoon ground cumin
3 pints (1.7 litres) celery stock	7½ cups celery stock
juice of 1 lemon	juice of 1 lemon
sea salt and black pepper	sea salt and black pepper

1
Melt the butter in a saucepan, add the lentils, onion and cumin and cook 2 minutes then add the vegetable stock and lemon juice.

2
Let simmer 20–30 minutes, when the lentils should be cooked through.

3
Let cool, then blend or put through a sieve. Reheat and garnish with any herbs available.

YELLOW SPLIT PEA SOUP

Turkey

Imperial (Metric)	American
½ lb (225g) yellow split peas	1 cup yellow split peas
2 oz (55g) butter	¼ cup butter
2 chopped onions	2 chopped onions
3 crushed cloves garlic	3 crushed cloves garlic
1 teaspoon ground cumin	1 teaspoon ground cumin
1 teaspoon ground coriander	1 teaspoon ground coriander
3 pints (1.7 litres) celery stock	7½ cups celery stock
juice of 1 lemon	juice of 1 lemon
2 tablespoons chopped parsley	2 tablespoons chopped parsley
sea salt and black pepper	sea salt and black pepper

1
Soak peas overnight then drain . Melt the butter in a saucepan, add the onion garlic, spices and peas; cook a few minutes.

2
Add the vegetable stock and simmer 1 hour or until peas are tender. Add more stock or water if peas are sticking to the bottom of the pan.

3
Let the soup cool and add the lemon juice.

4
Reheat and before serving add the parsley.

SPINACH SOUP

Turkey

Imperial (Metric)	American
1 lb (450g) fresh spinach leaves	2½ cups fresh spinach leaves
2 oz (55g) butter	¼ cup butter
2 tablespoons flour	2 tablespoons flour
3 pints (1.7 litres) celery stock	7½ cups celery stock
3 egg yolks	3 egg yolks
¼ pint (150ml) thick cream	⅔ cup heavy cream
2 tablespoons chopped parsley	2 tablespoons chopped parsley
sea salt and black pepper	sea salt and black pepper

1

Melt the butter in a saucepan, shred the spinach leaves and add them to
the pan. Place over low heat, covered, and let simmer 10 minutes.

2

Give the spinach a stir and sprinkle the flour over it. Continue to stir
allowing the flour to cook. After a minute or two add the celery stock and
simmer another 10 minutes.

3

Let the soup cool, then put through the blender, adding the egg yolks and
cream.

4

Reheat with care, adding the parsley at the last moment.

LABANEYA
Spinach Soup with Yogurt

Egypt

Imperial (Metric)	American
3 tablespoons olive oil	3 tablespoons olive oil
1 lb (450g) spinach leaves	2 cups (when cooked) spinach leaves
2 onions, chopped	2 onions, chopped
2 crushed garlic cloves	2 crushed garlic cloves
½ pint (285ml) yogurt	1⅓ cups yogurt
3 pints (1.7 litres) celery stock	7½ cups celery stock
4 spring onions, chopped	4 scallions, chopped
sea salt and black pepper	sea salt and black pepper

1
Heat the oil in a saucepan, chop the spinach and add it to the oil with the onion. Cover the saucepan and cook 10 minutes.

2
Add the garlic to the yogurt. Add the stock to the spinach and continue to cook another 10 minutes. Let cool, then blend the soup, adding the yogurt.

3
Reheat carefully, adding the spring onions (scallions). Taste and check for seasoning.

HOT CUCUMBER SOUP

Greece

Imperial (Metric)	American
1 lb (450g) potatoes	1 pound potatoes
2 onions	2 onions
2 pints (1.2 litres) celery stock	5 cups celery stock
2 cucumbers	2 cucumbers
1 pint (570ml) milk	2½ cups milk
sea salt and black pepper	sea salt and black pepper
handful chopped chives	handful chopped chives

1

Peel and dice the potatoes. Slice the onions and boil both in stock until tender.

2

When the soup is cool, blend to a thin purée and pour back into the saucepan.

3

Grate the cucumbers into the soup and add the milk. Taste, season and reheat carefully, adding the herbs at the last minute.

HOT BEAN SOUP

Morocco

Imperial (Metric)	American
2 oz (55g) borlotti beans	⅓ cup pinto beans
2 oz (55g) green lentils	⅓ cup green lentils
2 oz (55g) chickpeas	¼ cup garbanzos
3 dried red chilli peppers	3 dried red chili peppers
3 pints (1.7 litres) celery stock	7½ cups celery stock
2 tablespoons tomato purée	2 tablespoons tomato paste
½ pint (285ml) yogurt	1⅓ cups yogurt
3 crushed cloves garlic	3 crushed cloves garlic
juice and zest of 1 lemon	juice and zest of 1 lemon
sea salt and black pepper	sea salt and black pepper
3 tablespoons chopped mint	3 tablespoons chopped mint

1

Soak the beans, lentils and chickpeas (garbanzos) overnight. Drain and combine with celery stock and chilli peppers. Stir in the tomato paste and simmer 2 hours.

2

Combine garlic, yogurt and chopped mint with a little salt and pepper.

3

Take out half the soup and blend to a purée. Pour it back into the saucepan, taste and check for seasoning. Reheat the soup and serve with the yogurt on the table; this is stirred into individual bowls as desired.

BEETROOT (BEET) SOUP

Malta

Imperial (Metric)	American
1 lb (450g) raw beetroot	1 pound raw beets
2 onions, chopped	2 onions, chopped
2 red peppers, sliced	2 red peppers, sliced
5 fl oz (150ml) olive oil	$\frac{2}{3}$ cup olive oil
3 pints (1.7 litres) celery stock	$7\frac{1}{2}$ cups celery stock
2 crushed cloves garlic	2 crushed cloves garlic
juice of 1 lemon	juice of 1 lemon
sea salt and black pepper	sea salt and black pepper
$\frac{1}{2}$ pint (285ml) yogurt	$1\frac{1}{3}$ cups yogurt

1

Peel and dice beetroots (beets) and add with onion and pepper to the oil in a saucepan. Cook a few minutes then add the celery stock, garlic and lemon juice. Simmer 1 hour.

2

Let the soup cool, then blend. Taste and check for seasoning. Either chill the soup or reheat. It is eaten with yogurt at the table.

ALMOND SOUP

Tunisia

Imperial (Metric)	American
½ lb (225g) ground almonds	2 cups ground almonds
½ teaspoon ground coriander	½ teaspoon ground coriander
½ teaspoon ground cumin	½ teaspoon ground cumin
3 oz (85g) wholemeal breadcrumbs, fresh	1½ cups whole wheat breadcrumbs, fresh
2 crushed cloves garlic	2 crushed cloves garlic
½ pint (285ml) milk	1⅓ cups milk
1½ pints (850ml) vegetable stock	3¾ cups vegetable stock
sea salt and black pepper	sea salt and black pepper
½ pint (285ml) single cream	1⅓ cups light cream

1

Put the almonds, spices, breadcrumbs and garlic in a pan and slowly add the milk, stirring all the time. When it is quite smooth add the celery stock. Heat and simmer 10 minutes.

2

Remove from heat, season and stir in the cream. Serve.

MINESTRONE

Italy

Imperial (Metric)	American
5 fl oz (150ml) olive oil	$\frac{2}{3}$ cup olive oil
5 crushed cloves garlic	5 crushed cloves garlic
2 onions, chopped	2 onions, chopped
1 small green cabbage, chopped	1 small green cabbage, chopped
3 leeks, sliced	3 leeks, sliced
$\frac{1}{2}$ lb (225g) young carrots	$\frac{1}{2}$ pound young carrots
3 pints (1.7 litres) celery stock	$7\frac{1}{2}$ cups celery stock
3 oz (85g) wholewheat pasta	$1\frac{1}{2}$–2 cups whole wheat pasta
sea salt and black pepper	sea salt and black pepper
2 oz (55g) freshly grated	$\frac{1}{2}$ cup freshly grated
Parmesan	Parmesan

1
Heat the olive oil in a large pan and add the garlic and all the chopped vegetables. Let cook 5 minutes, then add stock and simmer a further 10 minutes; add the pasta and cook another 10 minutes.

2
Add the seasoning. Allow the soup to rest away from the heat 5 minutes before serving.

3
Be generous with the grated Parmesan.

SOPA DE GUISANTES Y PATATAS
Fresh Pea and Potato Soup

Spain

Imperial (Metric)	American
2 oz (55g) butter	$\frac{1}{4}$ cup butter
1 cos lettuce	1 cos lettuce
1 lb (450g) new potatoes	1 pound new potatoes
1 lb (450g) garden peas, shelled	$2\frac{2}{3}$ cups garden peas, shelled
3 pints (1.7 litres) vegetable stock	$7\frac{1}{2}$ cups vegetable stock
$\frac{1}{2}$ pint (285ml) single cream	$1\frac{1}{3}$ cups light cream
sea salt and black pepper	sea salt and black pepper

1

Melt the butter in a saucepan. Shred the lettuce, dice the potatoes and add with the peas to the butter. Cover the saucepan and simmer over low heat 5 minutes.

2

Add the vegetable stock, bring to a boil and simmer a further 15 minutes.

3

Let the soup cool and blend, adding the cream and seasoning. Reheat with care.

SOPA DE TOMATE, PATATA Y CEBOLLA
Tomato, Potato and Onion Soup

Spain

Imperial (Metric)	American
1 lb (450g) tomatoes	1 pound tomatoes
5 fl oz (150ml) olive oil	⅔ cup olive oil
½ lb (225g) onions, chopped	½ pound onions, chopped
½ lb (225g) potatoes, diced	½ pound potatoes, diced
3 pints (1.7 litres) celery stock	7½ cups celery stock
3 egg yolks, beaten	3 egg yolks, beaten
sea salt and black pepper	sea salt and black pepper

1
Slice the tomatoes in half and place them in a saucepan. Cover the pan and leave over very low heat 10 minutes. Pass the tomatoes through a sieve and reserve the sauce. Discard the skin and seeds (this is a basic sauce, used in other recipes).

2
Heat the olive oil in a saucepan and add the onions and potatoes. Cook a few minutes, add the stock and simmer another 20 minutes. Let the soup cool.

3
Blend the soup in a blender and add the tomato sauce. Reheat, adding a little of the hot soup to the egg yolks in a bowl then pouring the yolk mixture back into the soup. Continue to heat so that the soup thickens.

SOPA DE GUISANTES Y PUNTAS DE ESPARRÁGOS
Pea and Asparagus Soup

Spain

Imperial (Metric)	American
1 bunch asparagus	1 bunch asparagus
1 lb (450g) garden peas, shelled	2⅔ cups garden peas, shelled
2 tablespoons olive oil	2 tablespoons olive oil
3 pints (1.7 litres) vegetable stock	7½ cups vegetable stock
5 tablespoons tapioca	⅓ cup tapioca
sea salt and black pepper	sea salt and black pepper

1
Cut the tips off the asparagus and reserve. Heat the olive oil in a pan and cook the asparagus stalks and peas in it a few moments. Add the vegetable stock and simmer 15 minutes.

2
Blend the soup in a blender, then pass soup through a sieve discarding the fibre.

3
Reheat the soup and add the tapioca. Cook 5 minutes and then add the asparagus tips. Taste and season; simmer a further 6 or 7 minutes.

SOPA DE PURÉ DE VERDURAS
Vegetable Purée Soup

Spain

Imperial (Metric)	American
4 oz (100g) each of potatoes, carrots, turnips, leeks, cabbage and runner beans	¼ pound each of potatoes, carrots, turnips, leeks, cabbage and green beans
3 tablespoons olive oil	3 tablespoons olive oil
3 pints (1.7 litres) celery stock	7½ cups celery stock
2 egg yolks	2 egg yolks
sea salt and pepper	sea salt and black pepper

1

Dice all the vegetables and add to the olive oil in a saucepan. Cook a few moments then add the celery stock and simmer ½ hour.

2

Blend the soup in a blender and season to taste. Reheat and bind the soup by adding a little of the hot soup to the egg yolks and then pouring it all back into the remaining soup. Continue to heat until soup thickens.

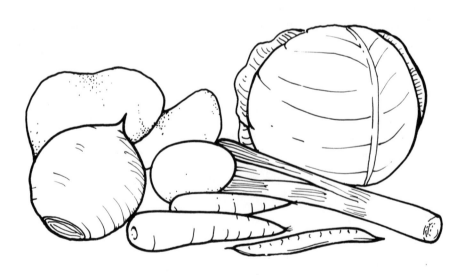

HARIRA

Morocco

Imperial (Metric)	American
2 oz (55g) each of the following: chickpeas, butter beans, black-eyed beans, red kidney beans,* green lentils, flageolets	¼–⅓ cup each of the following: garbanzos, lima beans, green lentils, flageolets, red kidney beans,* black-eyed beans
5 fl oz (150ml) olive oil	⅓ cup olive oil
2 oz (55g) peeled and shredded ginger root	½ cup peeled and shredded ginger root
1 teaspoon turmeric	1 teaspoon turmeric
1 teaspoon cinnamon	1 teaspoon cinnamon
½ lb (225g) chopped onions	1⅓ cups chopped onions
14 oz (400g) tin tomatoes	14-ounce can tomatoes
juice and zest of 2 lemons	juice and zest of 2 lemons
1½ tablespoons flour	1½ tablespoons flour
sea salt and black pepper	sea salt and black pepper
2 tablespoons chopped mint	2 tablespoons chopped mint
2 tablespoons fresh coriander	2 tablespoons fresh coriander
1 teaspoon paprika	1 teaspoon paprika

1

Soak all the beans and lentils overnight. Heat the olive oil in a large saucepan. Add the ginger root, spices and chopped onions. Cook a few moments then add the tomatoes, lemon juice and zest. Add 4 pints (2.3 litres) water, all the beans and lentils and simmer 2 hours.

2

Add 3 tablespoons cold water to the flour and mix to a paste. Pour into the paste some of the soup, stir well and pour it back into the saucepan. Cook another ½ hour or until all the beans are done. Season the soup and add the fresh herbs and paprika.

* See note on page 9.

SOUPE AUX TOMATES À L'ESTRAGON
Tomato Soup with Tarragon

Corsica

Imperial (Metric)	American
2 lb (900g) tomatoes, chopped	2 pounds tomatoes, chopped
2 oz (55g) butter	$\frac{1}{4}$ cup butter
2 tablespoons freshly chopped tarragon	2 tablespoons freshly chopped tarragon
1 tablespoon dried tarragon	1 tablespoon dried tarragon
5 crushed cloves garlic	5 crushed cloves garlic
1½ pints (850ml) vegetable stock	3¾ cups vegetable stock
sea salt and black pepper	sea salt and black pepper

1
Melt the butter and add the tomatoes, tarragon and garlic. Cover the pan and cook over low heat for 10 minutes.

2
Add the vegetable stock and seasoning, then continue to cook another 10 minutes.

3
Blend the soup and pass it through a sieve. Either reheat the soup and serve with soured cream or serve it chilled.

POTAGE DE POMMES DE TERRE ET POIREAUX
Potato and Leek Soup

France

Imperial (Metric)	American
1 lb (450g) potatoes	1 pound potatoes
1½ pints (850ml) water	3¾ cups water
1 lb (450g) leeks	1 pound leeks
2 oz (55g) butter	¼ cup butter
½ pint (285ml) milk	1⅓ cups milk
¼ pint (150ml) single cream	⅔ cup light cream
sea salt and black pepper	sea salt and black pepper
2 tablespoons finely chopped parsley	2 tablespoons finely chopped parsley

1
Peel the potatoes and boil them in the water until tender. Let them cool, place in a blender and purée.

2
Meanwhile trim and clean the leeks, chop them coarsely and cook them in the butter in a covered pan until they are soft, about 10 minutes.

3
Add these to the blender jar with the milk, cream and seasoning and blend to a thin purée. Return to the pan and reheat with care, adding the parsley at the last moment.

SOUPE À L'ARTICHAUT
Artichoke Soup

France

Imperial (Metric)	American
10 young baby artichokes	10 young baby artichokes
1½ pints (850ml) water	3¾ cups water
2 oz (55g) butter	¼ cup butter
2 tablespoons wholemeal flour	2 tablespoons whole wheat flour
½ pint (285ml) milk	1⅓ cups milk
5 fl oz (150ml) single cream	⅔ cup light cream
pinch of nutmeg	pinch of nutmeg
sea salt and black pepper	sea salt and black pepper

1
Trim the artichokes and discard any tough outside leaves. Boil them in the water 20 minutes. Let cool then blend them with their water to a thin purée.

2
Meanwhile melt the butter, add the flour, cook for a moment, then add the milk, cream and seasonings to make a white sauce.

3
Add the sauce to the artichoke purée and blend well. Return to the pan and reheat with care.

GARBURE BÉARNAISE

France

Imperial (Metric)	American
6 oz (180g) white haricot beans	1 cup white navy beans
3 pints (1.7 litres) water	7½ cups water
½ lb (225g) potatoes	½ pound potatoes
½ lb (225g) green beans	½ pound green beans
½ lb (225g) white cabbage	½ pound white cabbage
5 tablespoons olive oil	5 tablespoons olive oil
5 crushed cloves garlic	5 crushed cloves garlic
1 tablespoon chopped marjoram	1 tablespoon chopped marjoram
1 teaspoon dried oregano	1 teaspoon dried oregano
½ teaspoon cayenne pepper	½ teaspoon cayenne pepper
sea salt	sea salt

1

Soak the beans overnight in the water. Bring to a boil and cook 2 hours.

2

Peel and dice the potatoes, trim and cut the beans into chunks and slice the cabbage. Cook these in the olive oil in another pan with the garlic, marjoram, oregano and cayenne pepper about 5 minutes, then add the beans and their liquid and boil another 20 minutes. Check for seasoning before serving.

SOUPE À LA CITROUILLE
Pumpkin Soup

France

Imperial (Metric)	American
1½ lbs (680g) pumpkin flesh (without peel or seeds)	1½ pounds pumpkin flesh (without peel or seeds)
3 crushed cloves garlic	3 crushed cloves garlic
4 oz (100g) butter	½ cup butter
2 pints (1.2 litres) celery stock	5 cups celery stock
¼ pint (150ml) single cream	⅔ cup light cream
sea salt and black pepper	sea salt and black pepper

1

Cut the pumpkin flesh into chunks and cook it with the garlic in the butter in a covered pan about 10 minutes. Add the celery stock and cook another 10 minutes. Let cool.

2

Pour it into the blender jar and blend to a purée. Add cream and seasoning and reheat with care.

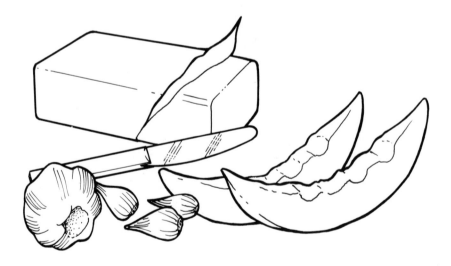

ZUPPA DI MARITATA

Italy

Imperial (Metric)	American
5 oz (140g) thin wholemeal noodles	1 cup thin whole wheat noodles
2 pints (1.2 litres) celery stock	5 cups celery stock
2 oz (55g) butter	$\frac{1}{4}$ cup butter
3 oz (85g) grated Parmesan	$\frac{3}{4}$ cup grated Parmesan
4 egg yolks	4 egg yolks
$\frac{1}{2}$ pint (285ml) thick cream	$1\frac{1}{3}$ cups heavy cream
sea salt and black pepper	sea salt and black pepper

1
Cook the noodles in the stock 15 minutes or until tender.

2
Mix the rest of the ingredients and gradually add some of the hot stock. Pour this back into the soup stirring all the time until the soup thickens a little. Serve immediately.

STRACCIATELLA

Italy

Imperial (Metric)	American
2 eggs, beaten	2 eggs, beaten
3 tablespoons grated Parmesan	3 tablespoons grated Parmesan
2 tablespoons wholemeal breadcrumbs	2 tablespoons whole wheat breadcrumbs
$\frac{1}{4}$ teaspoon nutmeg	$\frac{1}{4}$ teaspoon nutmeg
sea salt and black pepper	sea salt and black pepper
2 pints (1.2 litres) celery stock	5 cups celery stock
2 tablespoons finely chopped parsley	2 tablespoons finely chopped parsley

1

Mix the eggs, cheese, breadcrumbs, nutmeg and seasoning and stir in a $\frac{1}{4}$ pint (150ml) of the stock. Stir thoroughly.

2

Heat the rest of the stock and when simmering add the egg mixture, stirring constantly, so that the eggs marble the soup. Sprinkle in the parsley before serving.

SOPA DE BORONIA

Spain

Imperial (Metric)	American
5 fl oz (150ml) olive oil	⅔ cup olive oil
1 aubergine, cubed	1 eggplant, cubed
½ lb (225g) cantaloupe flesh, diced	½ pound cantaloupe flesh, diced
2 onions, chopped	2 onions, chopped
5 crushed cloves garlic	5 crushed cloves garlic
½ pint (285ml) tomato sauce (see page 104)	1⅓ cups tomato sauce (see page 104)
¼ teaspoon cayenne pepper	¼ teaspoon cayenne pepper
¼ teaspoon saffron	¼ teaspoon saffron
2 pints (1.2 litres) celery stock	5 cups celery stock
sea salt and black pepper	sea salt and black pepper
4 slices toasted wholemeal bread	4 slices toasted whole wheat bread
4 poached eggs	4 poached eggs

1

Heat the oil in a large pan and sauté the aubergine (eggplant) cubes about 5 minutes. Add the cantaloupe, onions and garlic, tomato sauce, cayenne pepper and saffron, season and cook another 10 minutes.

2

Add the stock, bring to a boil and let cook a further 10 minutes. Let it cool then blend to a purée.

3

Reheat the soup with care, put it into a tureen and lay the toasted bread on the surface with a poached egg on each piece.

SOPA DE ESPÁRRAGO Y AVELLANA
Asparagus and Hazelnut Soup

Spain

Imperial (Metric)	American
½ lb (225g) asparagus spears	½ pound asparagus spears
2 pints (1.2 litres) water	5 cups water
2 oz (55g) butter	¼ cup butter
4 oz (100g) shelled hazelnut kernels, finely chopped	¾ cup shelled hazelnut kernels, finely chopped
1 glass dry sherry	1 glass dry sherry
½ pint (285ml) single cream	1⅓ cups light cream
sea salt and black pepper	sea salt and black pepper

1

Cut the tips off the asparagus and reserve them. Boil the rest of the asparagus in the water about 15 minutes. Cool, then process in a blender and put through a sieve.

2

Melt the butter in the pan, add the hazelnuts, sauté 5 minutes until they have turned brown. Add the asparagus stock and bring to a boil. Add the asparagus tips and simmer 12 minutes.

3

Season the soup and add the sherry and cream, stir and reheat, but do not allow to boil.

SOPA DE GARBANZOS
Chickpea (Garbanzo) Soup

Spain

Imperial (Metric)	American
½ lb (225g) dried chickpeas	1 cup dried garbanzos
4 pints (2.3 litres) water	10 cups water
½ lb (225g) potatoes	½ pound potatoes
½ lb (225g) onions	½ pound onions
1 cos lettuce	1 cos lettuce
2 leeks	2 leeks
5 fl oz (150ml) olive oil	⅔ cup olive oil
5 cloves garlic	5 cloves garlic
1 teaspoon oregano	1 teaspoon oregano
½ teaspoon caraway seeds	½ teaspoon caraway seeds
sea salt and black pepper	sea salt and black pepper

1
Soak the chickpeas (garbanzos) overnight in the water. Bring them to a boil and let them simmer 2 hours.

2
Peel and dice the potatoes, slice the onions, lettuce and leeks. Heat the olive oil in another pan and cook all the vegetables with the garlic, oregano and caraway seeds about 5 minutes.

3
Pour half of the chickpeas (garbanzos) with their liquid into a blender and blend. Add this to the vegetables and olive oil with the whole chickpeas (garbanzos) and the rest of the water they were cooked in. Season the soup and cook a further 20 minutes.

CHILLED PARSLEY SOUP

Morocco

Imperial (Metric)	American
1 large bunch parsley	1 large bunch parsley
2 pints (1.2 litres) vegetable stock	5 cups vegetable stock
2 egg yolks	2 egg yolks
½ pint (285ml) yogurt	1⅓ cups yogurt
¼ teaspoon cayenne pepper	¼ teaspoon cayenne pepper
sea salt and parsley to garnish	sea salt and parsley to garnish

1

Simmer the parsley in the stock 20 minutes. Let it cool, then purée in the blender. Add the rest of the ingredients and blend again.

2

Chill thoroughly and check for seasoning before serving. Garnish with sprigs of parsley.

Chapter 5
Egg and Cheese Dishes

Eggs in Mediterranean food must begin with the classic omelette of France, though there is a whole section of dishes that derive from the omelette but are heavier and more substantial. Even in the south of France the plain classic omelette is often augmented with spoonfuls of various vegetables or their purées such as mushroom, onion, courgette (zucchini) or ratatouille. There is the Spanish tortilla, the Egyptian eggah and the Tunisian tagine — all these belong very much to hearty peasant fare rather than the original omelette, which must be light and insubstantial.

Omelette

France

This is best made individually using no more than three small eggs or two large ones. Use an omelette pan, shallow with sloping sides, make sure that it is quite smooth and clean and use a very small amount of butter, just enough to moisten the bottom of the pan. Do not beat the eggs but mix the yolks and white together with a few stirrings of a fork or spoon, add a teaspoon of cold water to lighten the mixture and a little seasoning. When the butter has begun to sizzle in the pan pour in the eggs. Pick up the pan and angle it, so that the eggs are evenly spread and keep a seesaw motion going so that the eggs are evenly set. It should take no longer than 45 seconds and with some assistance from a spoon the omelette will roll over onto itself and thence onto a warm plate. The centre should still be unset, a few freshly chopped herbs can be added once the eggs have been poured into the pan. The dish is simple yet is rarely done to perfection.

TORTILLA CLÁSICA
Classic Omelette

Spain

Imperial (Metric)	American
6 eggs	6 eggs
3 tablespoons chopped parsley	3 tablespoons chopped parsley
5 fl oz (150ml) cream	$\frac{2}{3}$ cup cream
1 oz (30g) butter	$2\frac{1}{2}$ tablespoons butter
sea salt and black pepper	sea salt and black pepper

1
In a bowl mix the eggs with the cream, parsley and seasoning.

2
Heat the butter in a shallow pan and pour in the eggs, angling the pan so that the egg covers the bottom evenly.

3
When it is almost done, but the top is still unset, fold each side toward the centre like an envelope and ease this envelope onto a warm plate.

TORTILLA DE PATATAS
Potato Omelette

Spain

Imperial (Metric)	American
½ lb (225g) potatoes	½ pound potatoes
3 tablespoons olive oil	3 tablespoons olive oil
6 eggs	6 eggs
5 fl oz (150ml) cream	⅔ cup cream
3 tablespoons chopped parsley	3 tablespoons chopped parsley
1 oz (30g) butter	2½ tablespoons butter
sea salt and black pepper	sea salt and black pepper

1
Peel and slice the potatoes thinly, heat the oil in a pan and sauté the potatoes until they are brown and crisp. Pour off any excess oil.

2
Mix the eggs, cream and parsley in a bowl, put the butter into the pan with the potatoes and when it is melted and hot pour the egg mixture over the potatoes. Angle the pan and let the eggs set.

3
Do not try to fold the omelette. The more substantial these Spanish omelettes are, the more they have to be served like wedges of cake.

TORTILLA CAMPESINA

Spain

Imperial (Metric)	American
2 chopped and seeded peppers	2 chopped and seeded peppers
2 chopped onions	2 chopped onions
1 chopped and seeded chilli	1 chopped and seeded chili
4 oz (100g) sliced mushrooms	1½ cups sliced mushrooms
3 peeled tomatoes	3 peeled tomatoes
3 crushed cloves garlic	3 crushed cloves garlic
juice of 1 lemon	juice of 1 lemon
6 eggs	6 eggs
4 tablespoons olive oil	4 tablespoons olive oil
3 tablespoons chopped parsley	3 tablespoons chopped parsley
sea salt and black pepper	sea salt and black pepper

1

Heat the oil in a wide shallow pan and sauté all the vegetables slowly with the lemon juice until they have amalgamated into a rough purée.

2

Mix the eggs, parsley and seasoning and pour over the cooked vegetables. Stir the egg mixture in and let the bottom set.

3

Place the pan under a hot grill for the top to rise and cook through. A minute, no more.

TORTILLA DE PATATAS Y CEBOLLA
Spanish Omelette with Potato and Onion

Spain

Imperial (Metric)	American
1 lb (450g) potatoes	1 pound potatoes
1 large onion	1 large onion
4 tablespoons olive oil	4 tablespoons olive oil
6 eggs	6 eggs
sea salt and black pepper	sea salt and black pepper

1

Peel and slice the potatoes thinly, chop the onions. Pour the olive oil into a pan and fry the potatoes and onion about 20 minutes.

2

Beat the eggs with the seasoning and when the potatoes are crisp and brown pour the egg mixture over them. Let the bottom set, then place the pan under a hot grill to allow the top to cook.

FRITTATA CON LE CIPOLLE
Italian Flat Omelette with Onions

Italy

Imperial (Metric)	American
3 large onions, sliced	3 large onions, sliced
2 tablespoons olive oil	2 tablespoons olive oil
5 eggs, beaten	5 eggs, beaten
sea salt and black pepper	sea salt and black pepper
1 oz (30g) butter	$2\frac{1}{2}$ tablespoons butter

1
Heat the olive oil in a frying pan and cook the onion over low heat about 10 minutes or until soft.

2
Have the eggs in a bowl and pour the onions into the eggs. Season well.

3
Melt the butter in the pan, pour the mixture in and proceed as for the preceding recipe.

FRITTATA AL FORMAGGIO
Italian Flat Omelette with Grated Cheese

Italy

Imperial (Metric)	American
6 eggs, beaten	6 eggs, beaten
3 oz (85g) freshly grated Parmesan	$\frac{3}{4}$ cup freshly grated Parmesan
1 oz (30g) Taleggio, cubed	2 tablespoons Taleggio, cubed
$1\frac{1}{2}$ oz (45g) butter	$\frac{1}{4}$ cup butter
sea salt and black pepper	sea salt and black pepper

1

Melt the butter in a frying pan. Add the Parmesan, salt and pepper to the eggs. Pour the mixture into the pan and strew the Taleggio over the top.

2

Let the omelette cook about 5 minutes so that the bottom is quite set and crisp, then finish cooking under a hot grill (broiler).

EGGAH

Egypt

Imperial (Metric)	American
2 oz (55g) of each of the following vegetables sliced thinly; courgettes, potatoes, onions, leeks, aubergines, mushrooms, spinach 4 crushed cloves garlic 4 tablespoons olive oil 8 eggs sea salt and black pepper 3 tablespoons freshly chopped parsley	$\frac{1}{3}$ to $\frac{1}{2}$ cup of each of the following, thinly sliced; zucchini, potatoes onions, leeks, eggplant $\frac{3}{4}$ cup mushrooms, thinly sliced 1 cup raw spinach, shredded 4 crushed cloves garlic 4 tablespoons olive oil 8 eggs sea salt and black pepper 3 tablespoons freshly chopped parsley

1

Heat the olive oil in a large shallow pan and cook all the vegetables with the garlic slowly — about 20 minutes or until they have become a thick mush.

2

Beat the eggs, seasoning and parsley together, pour over the vegetables and stir the mixture in. Let the bottom set, then finish the cooking by placing the pan under a hot grill (broiler). Slice like a cake.

TAGINE

Tunisia

Imperial (Metric)	American
2 peppers, cored and sliced	2 peppers, cored and sliced
2 courgettes, sliced	2 zucchini, sliced
2 onions, sliced	2 onions, sliced
1 lb (450g) tomatoes, peeled	1 pound tomatoes, peeled
5 crushed cloves garlic	5 crushed cloves garlic
5 fl oz (150ml) olive oil	$\frac{2}{3}$ cup olive oil
$\frac{1}{2}$ teaspoon each ground cumin, ground coriander and ground cinnamon	$\frac{1}{2}$ teaspoon each ground cumin, ground coriander and ground cinnamon
$\frac{1}{4}$ teaspoon each cayenne and nutmeg	$\frac{1}{4}$ teaspoon each cayenne and nutmeg
8 eggs	8 eggs
sea salt and black pepper	sea salt and black pepper

1

Preheat oven to 375°F/190°C (Gas Mark 5). Pour the oil into a large earthenware dish or marmite, cook all the vegetables and spices in the oil about 5 minutes or until they have begun to soften.

2

Mix eggs and seasoning and pour into the marmite, give a stir and bake in the oven about 40 minutes.

PIPERADE

France

Imperial (Metric)	American
3 peppers — red, green and yellow	3 peppers — red, green and yellow
2 large onions	2 large onions
4 tablespoons olive oil	¼ cup olive oil
5 crushed cloves garlic	5 crushed cloves garlic
1 lb (450g) tomatoes	1 pound tomatoes
sea salt and black pepper	sea salt and black pepper
6 eggs	6 eggs

1

Core and seed the peppers and slice them and the onion thinly into a large shallow pan, heat the oil and sauté the peppers, onions and garlic until they amalgamate into a purée, about 20 minutes.

2

Skin the tomatoes and add their pulp to the pan, raise the heat and let bubble about 5 minutes. Season with salt and pepper.

3

Beat the eggs and add them to the pan. Keep the heat high and mix egg and purée together with a fork as if you were making scrambled eggs.

4

Serve with garlic bread and a green salad.

CHAHCOUKA

Tunisia

Imperial (Metric)	American
4 tablespoons olive oil	¼ cup olive oil
4 crushed cloves garlic	4 crushed cloves garlic
3 peppers — red, green and yellow	3 peppers — red, green and yellow
2 chilli peppers	2 chili peppers
3 onions	3 onions
1 lb (450g) tomatoes	1 pound tomatoes
4 eggs	4 eggs
sea salt and black pepper	sea salt and black pepper

1
Pour the olive oil into a shallow pan and add the garlic. Seed and core the sweet peppers and slice peppers and onions thinly. Seed and slice the chilli peppers. Add all this to the olive oil and cook 15 minutes.

2
Peel the tomatoes and add them to the vegetable mixture, raise the heat a little, stir and continue to cook another 5 minutes.

3
Take away from the heat, make four depressions and break an egg into each. Return the pan to the heat and allow the whites to set.

OMELETTE À L'OSEILLE
Sorrel Omelette

France

Imperial (Metric)	American
1 oz (30g) butter	2½ tablespoons butter
3–4 sorrel leaves	3 or 4 sorrel leaves
3 eggs	3 eggs
sea salt and black pepper	sea salt and black pepper

1

Place half the butter in the pan and let it melt. Tear the stalks from the sorrel leaves, add the leaves to the butter and stir. They will reduce themselves to a purée within a couple of minutes. Pour into a bowl and reserve.

2

Put the rest of the butter into the pan, mix the eggs and pour into the pan. Now add the sorrel purée, allow it to set and fold the omelette in the normal way.

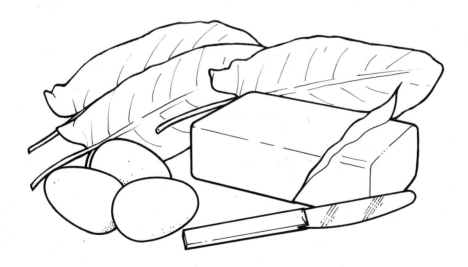

OMELETTE MOLIÈRE

France

Imperial (Metric)	American
3 eggs	3 eggs
1 tablespoon grated Parmesan	1 tablespoon grated Parmesan
1 tablespoon Gruyère, diced	1 tablespoon Gruyère, diced
1 tablespoon thick cream	1 tablespoon heavy cream
sea salt and black pepper	sea salt and black pepper
teaspoon butter	teaspoon butter

1

Mix the eggs with the Parmesan and season with salt and pepper. Melt the butter in a pan and pour the egg mixture into it.

2

Dot the omelette with the diced Gruyère and top with cream. As the Gruyère begins to melt fold the omelette over and serve.

PURSLANE OMELETTE

Greece

Imperial (Metric)	American
1 bunch of purslane	1 bunch of purslane
1 oz (30g) butter	2½ tablespoons butter
4 eggs	4 eggs
sea salt and black pepper	sea salt and black pepper

1

Cut the leaves off the purslane, melt the butter in a pan and cook the purslane leaves a few minutes.

2

Beat the eggs with the seasoning and pour into the pan. Let the omelette set and do not attempt to turn it, as it will break. Let it slip out of the pan and onto a warm plate.

OMELETTA ME DOMATES
Fresh Tomato Omelette

Greece

Imperial (Metric)	American
3 tablespoons olive oil	3 tablespoons olive oil
1 lb (450g) tomatoes	1 pound tomatoes
$\frac{1}{4}$ teaspoon oregano	$\frac{1}{4}$ teaspoon oregano
4 tablespoons freshly chopped basil	4 tablespoons freshly chopped basil
6 eggs	6 eggs
sea salt and black pepper	sea salt and black pepper

1

Pour the oil into a pan, peel and slice the tomatoes and cook them gently in the pan with the seasoning and oregano about 7 minutes.

2

Beat the eggs well and add. Sprinkle the fresh basil over the top and let the eggs set on the bottom, but allow the top to be quite runny.

3

Serve on a large platter surrounded by garlic bread.

AVOCADO OMELETTE

Israel

Imperial (Metric)	American
4 eggs	4 eggs
1 ripe avocado	1 ripe avocado
1 oz (30g) butter	2½ tablespoons butter
2 tablespoons chopped parsley	2 tablespoons chopped parsley
sea salt and black pepper	sea salt and black pepper

1
In a bowl beat the eggs, add the flesh of the avocado and go on beating until the mixture is smooth (for ease use an electric blender). Season the mixture.

2
Melt the butter in a pan and pour in the egg and avocado mixture, sprinkle with the chopped parsley and let the omelette set at the bottom of the pan.

3
Put the pan under a hot grill (broiler) to cook the top.

WALNUT OMELETTE

Lebanon

Imperial (Metric)	American
6 eggs	6 eggs
4 oz (100g) chopped walnuts	$\frac{3}{4}$ cup chopped walnuts
2 oz (55g) currants	$\frac{1}{3}$ cup currants
2 crushed cloves garlic	2 crushed cloves garlic
2 tablespoons chopped spring onions	2 tablespoons chopped scallions
$\frac{1}{2}$ teaspoon cumin	$\frac{1}{2}$ teaspoon cumin
2 tablespoons brown breadcrumbs	2 tablespoons brown breadcrumbs
3 tablespoons olive oil	3 tablespoons olive oil
sea salt and black pepper	sea salt and black pepper

1
Pour the oil into a pan, mix all the other ingredients together and add.
Heat to allow the omelette to set at the bottom.

2
Place the pan under a hot grill (broiler) to cook the top.

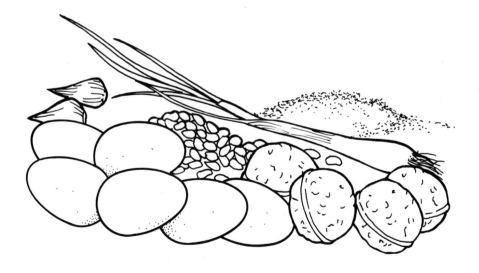

133

HUEVOS CON PURÉ

Spain

Imperial (Metric)	American
1 lb (450g) potatoes	1 pound potatoes
sea salt and black pepper	sea salt and black pepper
1 oz (30g) butter	2½ tablespoons butter
2 tablespoons milk	2 tablespoons milk
6 eggs	6 eggs

For the white sauce

Imperial (Metric)	American
1 oz (30g) butter	2½ tablespoons butter
1 oz (30g) wholemeal flour	¼ cup whole wheat flour
5 fl oz (150ml) milk	⅔ cup milk
pinch of salt and nutmeg	pinch of salt and nutmeg
5 fl oz (150ml) cream	⅔ cup cream

1

Peel and boil the potatoes until they are cooked. Drain well. Mash them with the butter, milk and seasoning to a smooth purée and make a layer of the purée in a well-buttered fireproof dish.

2

Make six depressions with the back of a spoon and break an egg into each.

3

Preheat oven to 375°F/190°C (Gas Mark 5). Sprinkle the eggs with a little salt and pepper and place in the oven for a few minutes while you make the white sauce.

4

Make a roux with the butter and the flour, add the milk, salt and nutmeg, pour in the cream. When it has become a smooth, thick sauce remove it from the heat.

5

Take the dish from the oven and if the whites are set, spoon the sauce over each egg and place under a hot grill to be lightly browned.

Soufflé

France

Like the omelette there are several Mediterranean dishes that stem from the classic French soufflé, most of them again rather more substantial than their parent. Yet all share the same factor of the eggs being separated and the whites whipped to beat in air so that the dish rises in the oven.

There is a myth that soufflés are difficult to make. It is untrue. Soufflés will always rise if the egg whites have been whipped enough for them to stand in peaks and the oven has been preheated to a hot enough temperature. All ovens are different and have their own idiosyncracies (for example, I find I get the best results cooking soufflés when using the oven of a wood burning stove where the exact temperature is a matter of guesswork) but usually the temperature that works best for a six-egg soufflé in an eight-inch (20 cm) soufflé dish will be 450°F/230°C (Gas Mark 7) for 15 to 18 minutes.

The best soufflés are made with no flour at all, not even the requisite one ounce that is in most recipes, and where the interior central part is still moist if not runny; therefore, it is important that soufflés should not be cooked right through and the old adage of sticking a knife in the centre and seeing if it comes out clean will only deflate the soufflé by letting the air out.

Soufflés are useful for using left over extra egg whites; in fact, most soufflés will respond better if they have two extra egg whites beaten into them. Some of the best soufflés are those that use vegetables in their purées such as spinach, sorrel, asparagus, and courgette (zucchini); they can all be made when once you have mastered the most classic soufflé of all, the simple cheese one given overleaf.

SOUFFLÉ AU FROMAGE
Cheese Soufflé

France

Imperial (Metric)	American
4 eggs	4 eggs
2 extra egg whites	2 extra egg whites
2 oz (55g) grated Parmesan	$\frac{1}{2}$ cup grated Parmesan
2 oz (55g) grated Gruyère	$\frac{1}{2}$ cup grated Gruyère
$\frac{1}{2}$ pint (285ml) single cream	$1\frac{1}{3}$ cups light cream
sea salt and black pepper	sea salt and black pepper
butter for the soufflé dish	butter for the soufflé dish

1
Thoroughly butter the inside of an 8-inch soufflé dish; preheat oven to
450°F/230°C (Gas Mark 8).

2
Have two mixing bowls with the 2 egg whites in one. Separate the eggs
and place all the whites together; the yolks go in the other bowl, to which
are added the grated cheeses, after which the cream and seasoning are
stirred in.

3
Whip the egg whites until they are stiff. Take about a third of the white
and fold into the cream mixture. You have to interleave the cream with the
froth. Continue with the rest of the egg white.

4
Have a hot baking sheet on the middle shelf of the oven. Pour the soufflé
into its dish and place it at once onto the baking sheet and leave 15–18
minutes. It is done when the top is risen and brown.

Note
Individual soufflés can be made in ramekins using this mixture; they will
only need between 8 and 10 minutes cooking.

SOUFFLÉ AUX COURGETTES
Courgette or Zucchini Soufflé

France

Imperial (Metric)	American
½ lb (225g) small courgettes	½ pound small zucchini
1 oz (30g) butter	2½ tablespoons butter
4 eggs	4 eggs
2 extra egg whites	2 extra egg whites
3 oz (85g) grated Gruyère	¾ cup grated Gruyère
½ pint (225g) single cream	1¼ cups light cream
sea salt and black pepper	sea salt and black pepper
butter for the soufflé dish	butter for the soufflé dish

1
Preheat the oven to 450°F/230°C (Gas Mark 8) and butter the soufflé dish well. Melt the butter in a pan and slice the courgettes (zucchini) thinly and add. Put a lid on the pan and let cook slowly 7–8 minutes. Let cool and put in a mixing bowl.

2
Separate the eggs and add the egg yolks to the courgettes (zucchini). Add the Gruyère, cream and seasoning.

3
Whip the egg whites until they are stiff and fold a third of them into the cream and courgette (zucchini) mixture; when that has been absorbed, fold in the rest.

4
Pour into the soufflé dish and place on a hot baking sheet in the middle of the oven; let cook 15–18 minutes.

Note
A Soufflé d'Aspèrge can be made using the same method with a bunch of cooked fresh asparagus.

SOUFFLÉ DI FINOCCHIO
Fennel Soufflé

Italy

Imperial (Metric)	American
3 heads fennel	3 heads fennel
4 eggs	4 eggs
2 extra egg whites	2 extra egg whites
2 oz (55g) each of Romano, Pecorino and Parmesan, all grated	½ cup each of Romano, Pecorino and Parmesan, all grated
½ pint (285ml) single cream	1⅓ cups light cream
sea salt and black pepper	sea salt and black pepper
butter for the soufflé dish	butter for the soufflé dish

1
Preheat the oven to 450°F/230°C (Gas Mark 8) and butter the soufflé dish well.

2
Cut away the green fronds from the fennel and reserve. Quarter the fennel roots and boil them in a little salted water 20 minutes. Drain well, blend the vegetable to a thick purée and pour it into a mixing bowl.

3
Separate the eggs and add the yolks, grated cheeses, cream and seasoning to the fennel purée; mix well.

4
Whip the egg whites until they are stiff, add a third of them to the other mixture and fold in. When this has been absorbed add the rest in the same manner.

5
Pour into the soufflé dish and place on a hot baking sheet in the middle of the oven; let cook 15–18 minutes.

6
Garnish with the chopped green fronds.

SOUFFLÉ DI FORMAGGIO
Italian Cheese Soufflé

Italy

Imperial (Metric)	American
4 eggs	4 eggs
2 extra egg whites	2 extra egg whites
2 oz (55g) grated Parmesan	$\frac{1}{2}$ cup grated Parmesan
2 oz (55g) Dolcelatte	$\frac{1}{4} - \frac{1}{2}$ cup Dolcelatte
2 oz (55g) Gorgonzola	$\frac{1}{4} - \frac{1}{2}$ cup Gorgonzola
2 oz (55g) Taleggio	$\frac{1}{4} - \frac{1}{2}$ cup Taleggio
$\frac{1}{2}$ pint (285ml) single cream	$1\frac{1}{3}$ cups light cream
sea salt and black pepper	sea salt and black pepper
butter for the soufflé dish	butter for the soufflé dish

Proceed as for the Soufflé au Fromage recipe. Except for the Parmesan, the Italian cheeses cannot be grated; ensure that they are ripe and cube them into the cream and egg yolks.

SOUFFLÉ FRITTO DI SPINACHI
Sautéed Spinach Soufflé

Italy

Imperial (Metric)	American
½ lb (225g) spinach leaves	½ pound spinach
1 oz (30g) butter	2½ tablespoons butter
1 oz (30g) wholemeal flour	¼ cup whole wheat flour
3 oz (85g) Bel Paese	⅓ cup Bel Paese
1 oz (30g) Parmesan	¼ cup Parmesan
4 eggs	4 eggs
sea salt and black pepper	sea salt and black pepper
Corn oil for frying	Corn oil for frying

1

Tear the spinach leaves from their stalks and place them in a saucepan with the butter, cover the pan and let the spinach cook slowly 10 minutes. Take the lid from the pan, raise the heat and drive off all the excess moisture. Take the pan from the flame.

2

Stir the flour into the spinach, and cook over a moderate flame 1 minute. Take away from the flame again and add the cheeses; let them melt a little, then pour them into a mixing bowl.

3

Separate the eggs and add the egg yolks to the spinach and mix well. Beat the egg whites until they are stiff and fold them into the egg mixture.

4

Pour about an inch (2.5cm) of oil into a shallow pan and heat it. When it is hot enough (test with a finger of bread and if it sizzles at once, it will be about right). Add the soufflé mixture in spoonfuls, about 4 at a time, turning them over so that they form balls. Drain them on absorbent paper.

EGGAH BI KORRAT
Leek Soufflé

Egypt

Imperial (Metric)	American
1 lb (450g) leeks	1 pound leeks
1 oz (30g) butter	2½ tablespoons butter
6 eggs	6 eggs
2 tablespoons olive oil	2 tablespoons olive oil
sea salt and black pepper	sea salt and black pepper

1
Trim and slice the leeks thinly. Cook them in a covered pan with the butter about 8 minutes then pour them into a mixing bowl.

2
Separate the eggs and add the beaten yolks to the leeks. Whip the egg whites until they are hard then fold them into the egg and leek mixture.

3
Heat the oil in a frying pan and pour in the soufflé omelette, let it cook slowly and finish by placing under a hot grill.

CAZUELA DE ESPINACAS CON HUEVOS A LA GRANADINA
Granada Spinach and Eggs

Spain

Imperial (Metric)	American
1 lb (450g) spinach leaves	2 cups spinach
½ teaspoon each saffron, cloves, peppercorns and cumin seeds	½ teaspoon each saffron, cloves, peppercorns and cumin seeds
3 tablespoons olive oil	3 tablespoons olive oil
3 oz (85g) peeled almonds	¾ cup peeled almonds
5 crushed cloves garlic	5 crushed cloves garlic
2 slices crustless wholemeal bread	2 slices crustless whole wheat bread
1 pint (570ml) celery stock	2½ cups celery stock
6 eggs	6 eggs
sea salt and black pepper	sea salt and black pepper

1
Take the spinach from the stalks and place leaves in a covered saucepan over low heat; let cook 10 minutes.

2
Place all the spices in a mortar and grind them to a powder; place in a bowl and add 1 tablespoon water to make a paste.

3
Pour the oil into a pan and sauté the almonds, garlic and bread until almonds are golden brown and the bread crisp. Place in a mortar and grind to a powder. This is more easily done in an electric blender.

4
Mix the spinach with the spices and the almond mixture; take a shallow fireproof dish and lay the spinach on the bottom. Heat the celery stock and pour over the spinach; mix well, so that it becomes a thick purée. Make 6 depressions in the purée and break the eggs into them. Sprinkle with sea salt and black pepper.

5
Have the oven pre-heated to 375°F/190°C (Gas Mark 5) and place the dish into it for 6 to 8 minutes or until the whites are set.

TIAN AUX POIREAUX

France

Imperial (Metric)	American
1½ lb (680g) leeks	1½ pounds leeks
2 oz (55g) butter	¼ cup butter
sea salt and black pepper	sea salt and black pepper
6 eggs	6 eggs
2 oz (55g) grated Gruyère	½ cup grated Gruyère
2 oz (55g) grated Parmesan	½ cup grated Parmesan

1

Clean, trim and slice the leeks thinly. Melt the butter in a saucepan, add the leeks and cook in a closed pan about 10 minutes, or until leeks are quite soft. Season and pour into a mixing bowl.

2

Add the beaten eggs and the cheeses. Butter a tian, or shallow earthenware dish. Preheat the oven to 350°F/180°C (Gas Mark 4) and bake in the oven about 30 minutes, or until the tian is risen and browned.

HUEVOS VERDOSO Y COLORADO

Green and Red Eggs

Spain

Imperial (Metric)	American
1 lb (450g) tomatoes	1 pound tomatoes
5 crushed cloves garlic	5 crushed cloves garlic
sea salt and black pepper	sea salt and black pepper
2 green peppers	2 green peppers
6 eggs	6 eggs

1

Place the tomatoes in a covered pan with the garlic and seasoning. Cook over low heat 10 minutes; let cool, then blend to a purée. Put the tomatoes through a sieve and pour the purée into a shallow earthenware dish.

2

Blister the outer skin of the green peppers over an open flame, scrape the skin away, then slice the tops from the peppers, core and seed them and cut them into thin strips.

3

Break the eggs into the tomato purée and lay the strips of green pepper over them. Sprinkle with sea salt and black pepper and place in a preheated 375°F/190°C (Gas Mark 5) oven 8 minutes or until the whites are set.

HUEVOS TORTOLA
Turtle Dove's Eggs

Spain

Imperial (Metric)	American
4 young globe artichokes	4 young globe artichokes
juice of 1 lemon	juice of 1 lemon
1 lb (450g) spinach leaves	1 pound spinach leaves
2 oz (55g) butter	$\frac{1}{4}$ cup butter
sea salt and black pepper	sea salt and black pepper
6 eggs	6 eggs
4 oz (100g) grated Manchego	1 cup grated Manchego

1
Make sure that the artichokes are really young, because they should have no choke in them. Cut them into quarters and boil them in a little salted water 10 minutes with the lemon juice.

2
Take the stalks from the spinach and cook the leaves in a covered pan over a low heat for 10 minutes. Drain any moisture from the spinach and chop it small with a wooden spoon.

3
Drain the artichokes carefully and add them to the spinach; mix in the butter and seasoning.

4
Butter a shallow fireproof dish and break the eggs into it, covering them with the spinach and artichokes. Sprinkle the cheese over the top, bake in a pre-heated 375°F/190°C (Gas Mark 5) oven 8–10 minutes.

TARTE AU FROMAGE

France

Imperial (Metric)	American
For the pastry:	
6 oz (170g) wholemeal flour	1½ cups wholewheat flour
3 oz (85g) butter	⅓ cup butter
½ teaspoon salt	½ teaspoon salt
2–4 tablespoons iced water	2 to 4 tablespoons iced water

Imperial (Metric)	American
For the béchamel sauce:	
1 oz (30g) butter	2½ tablespoons butter
2 tablespoons flour	2 tablespoons flour
5 fl oz (100ml) milk	⅔ cup milk
sea salt and black pepper	sea salt and black pepper
pinch cayenne pepper and nutmeg	pinch cayenne pepper and nutmeg

Imperial (Metric)	American
For the tarte:	
3 oz (85g) grated Gruyère	¾ cup grated Gruyère
2 oz (55g) grated Parmesan	½ cup grated Parmesan
4 tablespoons fromage frais (soft, low fat cheese)	4 tablespoons fromage frais (soft, low fat cheese)
2 eggs	2 eggs

1

To make the pastry, sieve the flour then grate the butter into it; add the salt and rub the butter into the flour. When a paste has formed, add enough iced water to make it smooth, roll into a ball, cover it in foil and refrigerate a few hours. Before using, bring it back to room temperature. Butter an eight or nine-inch flat pie or flan tin, smear the pastry over the bottom and up the sides, prick the flat surface with a fork, fill with dry beans and bake in a preheated 400°F/200°C (Gas Mark 6) oven 15 minutes.

2

Make the béchamel by melting the butter, adding the flour and letting it cook a little. Then slowly add the milk to make a thick sauce, season and add the cayenne and nutmeg, and stir in the Gruyère and Parmesan. Take away from the heat and when cool, stir in the fromage frais.

3

Separate the eggs, add the egg yolks to the cheese mixture and stiffly beat the whites. Fold the whites into the cheese mixture.

4

Take the beans from the pastry case and pour the cheese mixture into the tarte, bake in the oven at the same temperature used in Step 1 about 15 minutes, or until the filling has risen and is golden brown.

QUICHE AU FROMAGE BLANC

France

Imperial (Metric)	American
For the pastry:	
6 oz (170g) wholemeal flour	1½ cups whole wheat flour
3 oz (85g) butter	⅓ cup butter
½ teaspoon salt	½ teaspoon salt
2–4 tablespoons iced water	2 to 4 tablespoons iced water
For the filling:	
4 oz (100g) fromage blanc (soft, white cheese)	½ cup fromage blanc (soft, white cheese)
¼ pint (150ml) double cream	⅔ cup heavy cream
3 egg yolks	3 egg yolks
1 whole egg	1 whole egg
12 stoned black olives	12 pitted black olives
sea salt and black pepper	sea salt and black pepper

1

Make the pastry as for the preceding recipe.

2

Beat together the fromage blanc, cream, egg and extra egg yolks and season with salt and pepper. Pour this mixture into the pastry case and dot the surface with the black olives. Bake in a preheated 400°F/200°C (Gas Mark 6) oven 15 minutes.

FLAN DE POIREAUX À LA BARGEMON

Leek Flan Bargemon-style

France

Imperial (Metric)   *American*

(Pastry as for Tarte au Fromage)

Imperial (Metric)	American
1½ lb (680g) leeks	1½ pounds leeks
2 oz (55g) butter	¼ cup butter
12–18 stoned black olives	12–18 pitted black olives
3 egg yolks	3 egg yolks
1 whole egg	1 whole egg
½ pint (285ml) thick cream	1⅓ cups heavy cream
sea salt and black pepper	sea salt and black pepper

1

Make the pastry (see page 146).

2

Trim and slice the leeks and let them cook in the butter in a closed pan for 10 minutes.

3

Beat the egg yolks, whole egg and cream, season with salt and pepper, pour the leeks into the pastry case, dot with the olives and pour the egg-and-cream mixture over the top.

4

Bake in a preheated 400°F/200°C (Gas Mark 6) oven for 20 minutes.

PEPPER AND EGG TART

Spain

Imperial (Metric)	American
(Pastry as for Tarte au Fromage)	
3 red peppers	3 red peppers
2 onions	2 onions
5 crushed cloves garlic	5 crushed cloves garlic
¼ pint (150ml) olive oil	⅔ cup olive oil
1½ lb (680g) tomatoes	1½ pounds tomatoes
½ teaspoon each dried oregano and thyme	½ teaspoon each dried oregano and thyme
sea salt and black pepper	sea salt and black pepper
4 eggs	4 eggs

1
Divide the pastry into 6 tartlet cases and bake blind.

2
Chop the peppers and onions and add with the garlic to the olive oil. Let it cook over low heat 15 minutes.

3
Put the tomatoes into another saucepan and cook with the lid on for 10 minutes. Blend into a purée, then sieve. Discard the skin and pips (seeds), add the tomato purée to the pan with the oregano and thyme, season well and raise the heat, cooking a further 5 minutes.

4
Beat the eggs and make an omelette; roll the omelette up and cut into strips.

5
Fill the pastry cases with some of the tomato and pepper stew and decorate with a strip of egg.

TORTA DI POMODORO
Tomato Tart

Italy

Imperial (Metric)	American
2 lb (900g) tomatoes	2 pounds tomatoes
sea salt and black pepper	sea salt and black pepper
2–3 tablespoons cornmeal	2–3 tablespoons cornmeal
1 oz (30g) butter	2½ tablespoons butter
1 lb (450g) wholemeal puff pastry	1 pound whole wheat puff pastry
3 tablespoons grated Parmesan	3 tablespoons grated Parmesan
handful fresh basil, coarsely chopped	handful fresh basil, coarsely chopped

1

Cut the tomatoes into thick slices, season them with salt and pepper and roll the slices in the cornmeal. Melt the butter in a frying pan and sauté the tomato slices so that the cornmeal becomes crisp.

2

Roll out the pastry and line a 10 or 11-inch flan tin. Pile the tomato slices onto the pastry case and sprinkle the top with the Parmesan cheese and the basil.

3

Place in a preheated 450°F/230°C (Gas Mark 8) oven for 30 minutes.

STUFFED PANCAKES

Lebanon

Imperial (Metric)	American
1 egg	1 egg
½ lb (225g) wholemeal flour	2 cups whole wheat flour
½ pint (225ml) milk	1⅓ cups milk
1 tablespoon olive oil	1 tablespoon olive oil
3 oz (85g) Haloumi (hard salty cheese)	3 ounces Haloumi (hard salty cheese)
2 hard-boiled eggs	2 hard-cooked eggs
6 oz (170g) cottage cheese	¾ cup cottage cheese
sea salt and black pepper	sea salt and black pepper
corn oil for frying	corn oil for frying

1

Mix the raw egg with the flour and add the milk and olive oil to make a batter. Beat the batter well to get the air into it. Let it stand an hour and beat it again before using.

2

Lightly oil a frying pan and drip a tablespoon of batter into the pan to form small round pancakes, sauté on one side only. Remove from the pan and make the filling.

3

Cube the Haloumi and mash the hard-boiled eggs, stir into the cottage cheese with the seasoning.

4

Place 2 or 3 teaspoons of the mixture into the centre of the uncooked side of each pancake. Fold the pancakes over and press the edges together.

5

Add more corn oil to the frying pan and shallow fry the stuffed pancakes on both sides until brown.

CAULIFLOWER IN EGG AND MUSTARD SAUCE

Greece

Imperial (Metric)	American
1 medium-sized cauliflower	1 medium-sized cauliflower
6 hard-boiled eggs	6 hard-cooked eggs

For the sauce

Imperial (Metric)	American
2 tablespoons butter	2 tablespoons butter
1 small onion, or 3 shallots chopped	1 small onion, or 3 shallots chopped
3 oz (85g) chopped mushrooms	1–1¼ cups chopped mushrooms
2 tablespoons wholemeal flour	2 tablespoons whole wheat flour
½ pint (285ml) vegetable stock	1⅓ cups vegetable stock
½ pint (285ml) single cream	1⅓ cups light cream
sea salt and black pepper	sea salt and black pepper
1 tablespoon Dijon or Meaux mustard	1 tablespoon Dijon or Meaux mustard

1

Slice the cauliflower into separate florets, each with part of the stalk. Boil them in a little salted water about 4 minutes so that they are still al dente and drain them well.

2

Peel the eggs and slice 4 of them into quarters. Take a shallow fireproof dish and smear it with butter. Lay the quartered eggs at the bottom and put a layer of cauliflower over the top. Slice the other 2 eggs across and arrange those over the cauliflower.

3

Make the sauce. Cook the chopped onion or shallots with the mushrooms in the butter. Cover the pan and leave them 5 minutes, stir in the flour and let that cook for a moment then gradually add the stock and cream until you have a thick sauce. Now season it and stir in the mustard. Pour the sauce over the cauliflower and egg.

4

Place the dish in a preheated 400°F/200°C (Gas Mark 6) oven for 5 to 7 minutes.

SPINACH PANCAKES

Israel

Imperial (Metric)	American
4 eggs	4 eggs
2 tablespoons olive oil	2 tablespoons olive oil
4 oz (100g) wholemeal flour	1 cup whole wheat flour
5 fl oz (150ml) milk	$\frac{2}{3}$ cup milk
sea salt and black pepper	sea salt and black pepper
2½ lb (1.35kg) spinach	2½ pounds spinach
2 oz (55g) butter	$\frac{1}{4}$ cup butter
1½ oz (45g) wholemeal flour	$\frac{1}{3}$ cup whole wheat flour
5 fl oz (150ml) milk	$\frac{2}{3}$ cup milk
4 oz (100g) grated Parmesan	1 cup grated Parmesan
4 oz (100g) grated Cheddar	1 cup grated Cheddar
½ pint (285ml) sour cream	1$\frac{1}{3}$ cups sour cream

1
Mix the eggs with the olive oil and flour and add the milk and seasoning to make a thick batter.

2
Cook the spinach in a closed saucepan about 10 minutes. Raise the heat and take the lid off the pan to drive off any excess moisture. Chop the spinach roughly with a wooden spoon.

3
Melt the butter in the spinach and add the additional flour to make a roux. Cook for a moment then add the milk to make a thick sauce.

4
Make 12–15 pancakes, adding a little more milk to the mixture if the first pancake seems too thick. Drain them on absorbent paper (paper towels).

5
Butter a deep soufflé dish, lay a pancake at the bottom, cover it with spinach and sprinkle it with the Parmesan and cheddar. Continue, alternating the layers, ending with a pancake. Pour the sour cream over the top and sprinkle with a little more grated cheese. Bake in a preheated 400°F/200°C (Gas Mark 6) oven about 15 minutes or until the centre is bubbling.

EGG AND PEAS

Israel

Imperial (Metric)	American
2 lb (900g) garden peas	5⅓ cups garden peas, shelled
sprig of mint	sprig of mint
sea salt and black pepper	sea salt and black pepper
2 oz (55g) butter	¼ cup butter
7 eggs	7 eggs
5 fl oz (150ml) thick cream	⅔ cup heavy cream

1

Shell the peas and place them with the mint in a shallow pan with a little salted boiling water. Let them simmer 10 or 12 minutes or until tender. Drain off the liquid and add the butter to the pan.

2

Break 6 of the eggs over the peas in the pan and put back over the heat to cook.

3

Beat the other egg into the cream and pour over the eggs in the pan, season the dish and then place under a hot grill (broiler) for a moment or two before serving.

SCRAMBLED EGGS WITH MARROW (SUMMER SQUASH) FLOWERS

Malta

Imperial (Metric)	American
6 eggs	6 eggs
4–5 marrow or courgette flowers	4 or 5 summer squash or zucchini flowers
1 oz (30g) butter	2½ tablespoons butter
sea salt and black pepper	sea salt and black pepper

1
Beat the eggs with 1 tablespoon water and season them.

2
Trim the stalks from the flowers, melt the butter in a pan and sauté a few minutes. Add the eggs. Raise the heat and beat with a fork. Take away from the heat before the eggs are completely set.

HUEVOS BÉCHAMEL EMPANDAS

Spain

Imperial (Metric)	American
4 eggs	4 eggs
2 oz (55g) brown breadcrumbs	1 cup fresh brown breadcrumbs
sea salt and black pepper	sea salt and black pepper
2 oz (55g) butter	$\frac{1}{4}$ cup butter
2 oz (55g) flour	$\frac{1}{2}$ cup flour
$\frac{1}{2}$ pint (285ml) milk	$1\frac{1}{3}$ cups milk
1 beaten egg	1 beaten egg
corn oil for frying	corn oil for frying

1
Boil the 4 eggs mollet (about 5 minutes) then plunge them into cold water. Peel them and put aside.

2
Make a béchamel sauce with the butter, flour, milk and seasoning. Let it cool.

3
Roll the eggs in the béchamel sauce so that they are covered by a thin layer. Dip each one in the beaten egg and roll in breadcrumbs.

4
Sauté in the corn oil so that the outsides are crisp.

HUEVOS ARRIBA ESPAÑA

Spain

Imperial (Metric)	American
6 cloves garlic	6 cloves garlic
5 fl oz (150ml) olive oil	⅔ cup olive oil
4 slices wholemeal bread	4 slices whole wheat bread
4 eggs	4 eggs
2 oz (55g) Manchego cheese, grated	½ cup Manchego cheese, grated
pinch of cayenne	pinch of cayenne
sea salt and black pepper	sea salt and black pepper

1

Crush the garlic into a frying pan, add a little olive oil and sauté each slice of bread until it is crisp. They will soak up an enormous amount of oil. Lay each piece of bread on a baking tin.

2

Separate the eggs and place each yolk upon the fried bread. Whip the whites until they are stiff and mix in the grated cheese, cayenne and seasoning.

3

Cover the yolks with a generous spoonful of the white and bake in a preheated 400°F/200°C (Gas Mark 6) oven 10 minutes.

OEUFS À LA CRÉCY

France

Imperial (Metric)	American
1 lb (450g) young cooked carrots	1 pound young cooked carrots
juice and zest of 1 orange	juice and zest of 1 orange
2 egg yolks	2 egg yolks
6 mollet eggs	6 mollet eggs
1 oz (30g) butter	2½ tablespoons butter
1 oz (30g) flour	¼ cup flour
½ pint (285ml) milk	1⅓ cups milk
3 bay leaves	3 bay leaves
sea salt and black pepper	sea salt and black pepper

1

Place the carrots in a blender with the juice and zest of the orange and the egg yolks, add a little seasoning and blend until you have a purée. Pour that into a shallow earthenware dish.

2

Shell the eggs mollet and place them on the carrot purée; keep warm in a low oven.

3

Melt the butter in a pan and make a roux with the flour, add the milk and bay leaves and stir until you have a smooth sauce. Discard the bay leaves and pour the sauce over the eggs. Place under a hot grill a few minutes.

OEUFS DUR SOUBISE

France

Imperial (Metric)	American
1 lb (450g) onions	1 pound onions
2 oz (55g) butter	$\frac{1}{4}$ cup butter
1 oz (30g) wholemeal flour	$\frac{1}{4}$ cup whole wheat flour
5 fl oz (150ml) milk	$\frac{2}{3}$ cup milk
sea salt and black pepper	sea salt and black pepper
4 hard-boiled eggs	4 hard-cooked eggs

1

Slice the onions thinly and cook them in the butter in a closed pan 10 minutes. Add the seasoning and sprinkle in the flour, allowing the flour to cook for a moment or two then add the milk to make a thick sauce.

2

Peel and halve the eggs, place them at the bottom of an earthenware dish that has been well buttered, cover with the onion sauce and bake in a preheated 400°F/200°C (Gas Mark 6) oven 10 minutes.

SPINACH TIMBALE

France

Imperial (Metric)	American
1 oz (30g) butter	2½ tablespoons butter
2 oz (55g) fresh breadcrumbs	1 cup fresh breadcrumbs
½ lb (225g) spinach	½ pound spinach
chopped onion	chopped onion
2 oz (55g) mild cheese (such as Gruyère), grated	¼ cup mild cheese (such as Gruyère), grated
pinch of nutmeg	pinch of nutmeg
sea salt and black pepper	sea salt and black pepper
5 eggs	5 eggs
½ pint (285ml) milk	1⅓ cups milk
butter for the soufflé dish	butter for the soufflé dish

1

Butter a soufflé dish and sprinkle the bottom and sides with some of the breadcrumbs. Preheat the oven to 350°F/180°C (Gas Mark 4).

2

Cook the spinach in a covered pan 5 minutes then place in the electric blender and make a purée.

3

Cook the onion in the butter until soft, place in a mixing bowl with the spinach purée, cheese, nutmeg, seasoning and the remaining breadcrumbs. Beat the eggs into this mixture.

4

Heat the milk and add it slowly, beating the mixture as you pour. Put the resulting custard into the soufflé dish. Stand the dish in a baking tin of boiling water and place in the oven 45 minutes.

5

Let the custard settle for 5 minutes after taking it out of the oven, then invert it onto a warm platter. It can be served with a tomato sauce.

SFORMATO DI ZUCCHINI
Courgette or Zucchini Timbale

Italy

Imperial (Metric)	American
1½ lb (680g) courgettes	1½ pounds zucchini
3 oz (85g) butter	⅓ cup butter
2 tablespoons wholemeal flour	2 tablespoons whole wheat flour
½ pint (285ml) single cream	1⅓ cups light cream
2 oz (55g) Taleggio, cubed	½ cup Taleggio, cubed
2 oz (55g) Parmesan, grated	½ cup Parmesan, grated
sea salt and black pepper	sea salt and black pepper
6 eggs	6 eggs

1

Slice the courgettes (zucchini) and cook them in a pan with the butter about 10 minutes, or until they are soft. Work the flour into the mixture and cook a moment or two. Add the cream slowly and then the two cheeses. Continue to cook a minute or until the cheeses are melted. Take away from the flame.

2

Butter a soufflé dish or charlotte mould. Season the mixture and when cool beat it with the 6 eggs. Pour the mixture into the mould and cook in a preheated 350°F/180°C (Gas Mark 4) oven in a bain marie about 40 minutes.

PAPETON D'AUBERGINES

France

Imperial (Metric)	American
5 or 6 spinach leaves	5 or 6 spinach leaves
1½ lb (680g) aubergines	1½ pounds eggplant
salt	salt
1 large onion	1 large onion
5 tablespoons olive oil	5 tablespoons olive oil
3 crushed cloves garlic	3 crushed cloves garlic
1 teaspoon oregano	1 teaspoon oregano
sea salt and black pepper	sea salt and black pepper
4 eggs	4 eggs
5 fl oz (150ml) single cream	⅔ cup light cream
1½ lb (680g) tomatoes	1½ pounds tomatoes

1

Blanch the spinach leaves for a moment. Peel the aubergines (eggplant), cut them, sprinkle salt over them and leave 30 minutes. Butter a soufflé dish or charlotte mould. Line it with the blanched spinach leaves, leaving enough at the top to fold over and so enclose the mould completely.

2

Slice the onion. Rinse the excess salt off the aubergines (eggplant) and pat them dry. Melt the oil in a pan and sauté the sliced onion, aubergines (eggplant) and crushed garlic with the oregano about 20 minutes, or until it is all soft. Cool. Then blend to a purée.

3

Pour into a mixing bowl. Beat and add the eggs and cream. Taste for seasoning and add more if needed. Pour the purée into the lined soufflé dish or charlotte mould. Fold over the spinach leaves. Bake in a preheated 350°F/180°C (Gas Mark 4) oven in a bain marie about 45 to 50 minutes. Take out of the oven and leave to rest about 10 minutes before unmoulding.

4

Make the tomato sauce by cooking all the tomatoes in a covered pan 10 minutes, adding seasoning, then blending and sieving.

Chapter 6
Pasta and Rice Dishes

SPAGHETTI CON AGLIO E OLIO
Spaghetti with Oil and Garlic

Sicily

Imperial (Metric)	*American*
¾ lb (340g) wholemeal spaghetti	12 ounces whole wheat spaghetti
5 tablespoons olive oil	5 tablespoons olive oil
10 cloves garlic, finely chopped	10 cloves garlic, finely chopped
sea salt and black pepper	sea salt and black pepper
4 tablespoons finely chopped parsley	4 tablespoons finely chopped parsley

1

Boil the spaghetti in a large pan of salted water until it is just al dente. It should be done in about 8 or 10 minutes. Drain well and keep warm.

2

In another pan heat the oil and add the garlic; let it cook for a moment before tipping in the spaghetti. Stir vigorously so that the spaghetti is completely coated by the oil. Season, sprinkle with the parsley and give another stir before serving.

SPAGHETTI ALLA RUSTICA
Rural Spaghetti

Italy

Imperial (Metric)	American
2 lb (900g) fresh tomatoes	2 pounds fresh tomatoes
5 fl oz (150ml) olive oil	$\frac{2}{3}$ cup olive oil
5 crushed cloves garlic	5 crushed cloves garlic
5 tablespoons chopped fresh basil	5 tablespoons chopped fresh basil
sea salt and black pepper	sea salt and black pepper
1 lb (450g) wholemeal spaghetti	1 pound whole wheat spaghetti
5 oz (140g) freshly grated Parmesan	$1\frac{1}{4}$ cups freshly grated Parmesan

1

Place the tomatoes, olive oil and garlic with a little seasoning into a pan. Place the lid on and cook over low heat 10 minutes. Pour into a blender, add the fresh basil and process to a purée. Put this through a sieve and return it to the saucepan to reheat.

2

Meanwhile boil the spaghetti in lots of salted water. When it is done place in a warm serving bowl, pour the hot sauce over and scatter half of the cheese over the top, keeping the remaining half for the table to be used at people's discretion.

SPAGHETTI ALLA PUTTANESCA
Spaghetti with Olives, Capers and Tomatoes

Southern Italy

Imperial (Metric)	American
¼ pint (150ml) olive oil	⅔ cup olive oil
3 oz (85g) butter	⅓ cup butter
1 lb (450g) tomatoes	1 pound tomatoes
6 cloves garlic	6 cloves garlic
4 tablespoons capers	4 tablespoons capers
3 oz (85g) black olives, stoned and halved	¾ cup black olives, pitted and halved
sea salt and black pepper	sea salt and black pepper
¾ lb (340g) spaghetti	12 ounces spaghetti
3 tablespoons finely chopped parsley	3 tablespoons finely chopped parsley

1

Heat the oil and butter in a large frying pan, quarter the tomatoes and cook them with the garlic and capers about 5 minutes. Season and scatter the olives over the top.

2

Boil the spaghetti in lots of salted water; when it is al dente drain and pour into a warm serving dish. Pour on the sauce and sprinkle with the parsley.

SPAGHETTI AL PEPERONI
Spaghetti with Peppers

Italy

Imperial (Metric)	American
1 lb (450g) mixed red and yellow peppers	1 pound mixed red and yellow peppers
2 onions, finely sliced	2 onions, finely sliced
5 tablespoons olive oil	5 tablespoons olive oil
1 lb (450g) tomatoes, roughly chopped	1 pound tomatoes, roughly chopped
sea salt and black pepper	sea salt and black pepper
$\frac{3}{4}$ lb (340g) wholemeal spaghetti	12 ounces whole wheat spaghetti

1

Place the peppers under a hot grill to blister their skins. When they are cool peel, core and seed them.

2

Pour the olive oil into a pan and cook the onion until soft. Slice the peppers and add them to the pan; cook a further 3 or 4 minutes then add the tomatoes. Season and cook another 10 minutes.

3

Boil the spaghetti in lots of salted water; when it is al dente drain and pour into a warm serving dish. Pour on the sauce.

PENNE AL QUATTRO FORMAGGI
Pasta with Four Cheeses

Northern Italy

Imperial (Metric)	American
¾ lb (340g) wholemeal penne	12 ounces whole wheat penne
3 oz (85g) butter	⅓ cup butter
2 oz (55g) grated Parmesan	½ cup grated Parmesan
3 oz (85g) grated Gruyère	¾ cup grated Gruyère
3 oz (85g) Bel Paese, diced	½ cup Bel Paese, diced
3 oz (85g) Mozzarella, diced	½ cup Mozzarella, diced
sea salt and black pepper	sea salt and black pepper

1

Cook the pasta in salted water 15 to 18 minutes or until al dente. Drain well. Return the pasta to the warm saucepan and add half of the butter and half of the Parmesan. Add all of the other cheeses, season and mix well.

2

Butter a shallow fireproof dish and pour the pasta into it. Add the remaining butter and sprinkle with the rest of the Parmesan.

3

Bake in a preheated 400°F/200°C (Gas Mark 6) oven 15 minutes.

FETTUCCINE ALL'ALFREDO

Italy

Imperial (Metric)	American
¾ lb (340g) wholemeal fettuccine	12 ounces whole wheat fettuccine
2 oz (55g) butter	¼ cup butter
½ pint (285ml) double cream	1⅓ cups heavy cream
4 oz (100g) grated Parmesan cheese	1 cup grated Parmesan cheese
sea salt and black pepper	sea salt and black pepper

1

Cook the pasta in salted water for 15 to 18 minutes or until al dente. Put the butter and cream in a shallow fireproof dish and heat gently. Drain the pasta and pour it into the sauce; season with lots of black pepper and a little salt. Sprinkle with Parmesan cheese.

2

Place under a hot grill a few minutes before serving.

TORTIGLIONI AL GORGONZOLO
Spiral Pasta with Gorgonzola Sauce

Italy

Imperial (Metric)	American
¾ lb (340g) wholemeal tortiglioni	12 ounces whole wheat tortiglioni
5 fl oz (150ml) single cream	⅔ cup light cream
2 oz (55g) butter	¼ cup butter
sea salt and black pepper	sea salt and black pepper
5 oz (140g) Gorgonzola, cubed	¾ cup Gorgonzola, cubed
2 oz (55g) grated Parmesan	½ cup grated Parmesan

1

Cook the pasta in plenty of boiling, salted water until it is al dente, about 15 to 18 minutes. Put the cream, butter and seasoning with the Gorgonzola into a shallow fireproof dish and stir over a low heat until you have a smooth sauce.

2

Thoroughly drain the pasta, add it to the sauce and toss thoroughly. Sprinkle the grated Parmesan over the top and place under a hot grill (broiler) for a moment.

PASTICCIO DI LASAGNE ALLA SAINT MARTIN
Baked Lasagne with Mushrooms and Cheeses

Italy

Imperial (Metric)	American
1 lb (450g) wholemeal lasagne	1 pound whole wheat lasagne
1 lb (450g) mushrooms, thinly sliced	6 cups thinly sliced mushrooms
5 crushed cloves garlic	5 crushed cloves garlic
2 oz (55g) butter	¼ cup butter
sea salt and black pepper	sea salt and black pepper
5 oz (140g) Bel Paese, cubed	1 cup Bel Paese, cubed
5 oz (140g) Gruyère cheese, cubed	1 cup Gruyère cheese, cubed
6 oz (170g) freshly grated Parmesan	1½ cups freshly grated Parmesan
½ pint (285ml) double cream	1⅓ cups heavy cream

1
Boil the lasagne 15 to 20 minutes. Drain well and line a buttered fireproof dish or baking tin with the strips.

2
Melt the butter in a pan and cook the mushrooms and garlic over a low heat 10 minutes. Season and pour over the lasagne. Scatter the Bel Paese and Gruyère cheeses in between the mushrooms, sprinkle half of the Parmesan over the top.

3
Cover the top with another layer of lasagne and pour the cream over this with the rest of the lasagne.

4
Bake in a preheated 400°F/200°C (Gas Mark 6) oven 20 to 30 minutes or until the top is brown and bubbling.

ALCOCHOFAS CON ARROZ
Green Artichoke Paella

Spain

Imperial (Metric)	American
6 young artichokes	6 young artichokes
5 tomatoes	5 tomatoes
1 onion	1 onion
5 crushed cloves garlic	5 crushed cloves garlic
5 fl oz (150ml) olive oil	$\frac{2}{3}$ cup olive oil
$\frac{1}{2}$ lb (225g) brown rice	1 cup brown rice
sea salt and black pepper	sea salt and black pepper
pinch of saffron	pinch of saffron
1$\frac{1}{2}$ pints (850ml) celery stock	3$\frac{3}{4}$ cups celery stock

1
Trim and quarter the artichokes, slice the tomatoes and onion, put the garlic into the oil in a pan and add the vegetables. Sauté about 2 minutes then add the rice, seasoning and saffron. Cook a further 2 minutes. Pour in the celery stock and stir.

2
Bake in a preheated 375°F/190°C (Gas Mark 5) oven 45 minutes.

ARROZ A LA PRIMAVERA
Spring Rice

Spain

Imperial (Metric)	American
1 cauliflower	1 cauliflower
1 lb (450g) peas in their pods	1 pound peas in their pods
6 young artichokes	6 young artichokes
5 fl oz (150ml) olive oil	⅔ cup olive oil
2 oz (55g) butter	¼ cup butter
½ lb (225g) brown rice	1 cup brown rice
sea salt and black pepper	sea salt and black pepper
1½ pints (850ml) vegetable stock	3¾ cups vegetable stock

1

Shell the peas, break the cauliflower into florets, trim and quarter the artichokes. Boil the vegetables in a little salted water 5 minutes. Drain.

2

Melt the oil and butter in a large pan, add the vegetables and the rice; stir well, then pour in the vegetable stock.

3

Bake in a preheated 375°F/190°C (Gas Mark 5) oven 45 minutes.

ARROZ CON GARBANZOS
Rice with Chickpeas (Garbanzos)

Spain

Imperial (Metric)	American
5 fl oz (150ml) olive oil	$\frac{2}{3}$ cup olive oil
2 onions, sliced	2 onions, sliced
6 crushed cloves garlic	6 crushed cloves garlic
1 green chilli, deseeded and sliced	1 green chili pepper, seeded and sliced
2 green peppers, seeded and sliced	2 green bell peppers, seeded and sliced
$\frac{1}{2}$ lb (225g) brown rice	1 cup brown rice
$1\frac{1}{2}$ pints (850ml) celery stock	$3\frac{3}{4}$ cups celery stock
$\frac{1}{2}$ lb (225g) chickpeas, soaked overnight	1 cup garbanzos, soaked overnight
sea salt and black pepper	sea salt and black pepper
4 eggs, beaten	4 eggs, beaten
2 tablespoons chopped parsley	2 tablespoons chopped parsley

1

Pour the oil into a large pan, add the onion, garlic, chilli and peppers, cook a few moments then add the rice and celery stock. Bake in a preheated 375°F/190°C (Gas Mark 5) oven 45 minutes.

2

Meanwhile soak the chickpeas (garbanzos) and have them boiling in plenty of salted water 2 hours. When they are done, drain well and when the rice is cooked add them to the paella. Keep the dish warm.

3

Pour the eggs over the dish and place it back in the oven long enough for the eggs to cook through, a matter of minutes; sprinkle with the chopped parsley before serving.

PASTITSIO
Macaroni Pie

Greece

Imperial (Metric)	American
1 lb (450g) tomatoes	1 pound tomatoes
6 crushed cloves garlic	6 crushed cloves garlic
2 tablespoons chopped basil	2 tablespoons chopped basil
3 tablespoons olive oil	3 tablespoons olive oil
$\frac{3}{4}$ lb (340g) wholemeal macaroni	3 cups whole wheat macaroni
2 oz (55g) butter	$\frac{1}{4}$ cup butter
4 oz (100g) Feta cheese	$\frac{1}{3}$ cup Feta cheese
sea salt and black pepper	sea salt and black pepper
$\frac{1}{2}$ pint (285ml) béchamel sauce	1$\frac{1}{3}$ cups béchamel sauce
(see page 146)	(see page 146)

1

Cook the tomatoes, garlic and olive oil in a pan with a tightly fitting lid.
Place in a blender, add the basil and a little seasoning and purée, then
sieve it and reserve.

2

Boil the macaroni in salted water about 20 minutes, drain well, return to
the saucepan and add the butter and cheese. Toss and mix well.

3

Butter a deep earthenware dish, place half the béchamel sauce in the
bottom, put half the macaroni in and cover with half of the tomato sauce
then do the same with the other half of the ingredients.

4

Bake in a preheated 400°F/200°C (Gas Mark 6) oven 30 to 40 minutes.

RISOTTO CON SPINACI
Spinach Risotto

Italy

Imperial (Metric)	American
3 oz (85g) butter	$\frac{1}{3}$ cup butter
3 tablespoons olive oil	3 tablespoons olive oil
3 crushed cloves garlic	3 crushed cloves garlic
2 onions, finely chopped	2 onions, finely chopped
1 lb (450g) spinach leaves	1 pound spinach leaves
$\frac{3}{4}$ lb (340g) brown rice	$1\frac{1}{2}$ cups brown rice
$1\frac{1}{2}$ pints (850ml) vegetable stock	$3\frac{3}{4}$ cups vegetable stock
sea salt and black pepper	sea salt and black pepper
2 oz (55g) grated Parmesan	$\frac{1}{2}$ cup grated Parmesan

1
Melt the butter and olive oil in a large pan, add the garlic and onion and let it cook a few minutes.

2
Take the stalks from the spinach and discard, chop the leaves; add these to the oil and cook a few moments more or until the spinach is reduced by at least two thirds. Now add the rice and cook a few more minutes, stirring so that it does not stick to the pan.

3
Add half of the stock and simmer in a closed pan 30 minutes. Add more stock if the rice is drying out while still uncooked, but on no account let the rice get mushy.

4
Taste and check for seasoning, then stir in the Parmesan cheese before serving.

SULTANS PILAV

Turkey

Imperial (Metric)	American
2 oz (55g) butter	$\frac{1}{4}$ cup butter
4 tablespoons olive oil	4 tablespoons olive oil
$\frac{3}{4}$ lb (340g) brown rice	$1\frac{1}{2}$ cups brown rice
1 pint (570ml) vegetable stock	$2\frac{1}{2}$ cups vegetable stock
2 oz (55g) sultanas	$\frac{1}{3}$ cup golden seedless raisins
2 oz (55g) currants	$\frac{1}{3}$ cup currants
$\frac{1}{2}$ teaspoon cumin	$\frac{1}{2}$ teaspoon cumin
2 oz (55g) pistachios, chopped	$\frac{1}{2}$ cup pistachios, chopped
2 oz (55g) walnuts, chopped	$\frac{1}{2}$ cup walnuts, chopped
pinch of saffron	pinch of saffron
sea salt and black pepper	sea salt and black pepper

1

Melt the butter and oil in a large saucepan and add the rice, cumin and saffron and stir, cooking a few moments.

2

Add the rest of the ingredients, cover the pan and cook 40 to 45 minutes.

VERMICELLI PILAV

Lebanon

Imperial (Metric)	American
2 oz (55g) butter	$\frac{1}{4}$ cup butter
3 tablespoons olive oil	3 tablespoons olive oil
1 onion, chopped	1 onion, chopped
3 crushed cloves garlic	3 crushed cloves garlic
2 oz (55g) sultanas	$\frac{1}{3}$ cup golden seedless raisins
4 oz (100g) vermicelli	2 cups broken vermicelli
$\frac{1}{2}$ lb (225g) brown rice	1 cup brown rice
$1\frac{1}{2}$ pints (850ml) vegetable stock	$3\frac{3}{4}$ cups vegetable stock
sea salt and black pepper	sea salt and black pepper

1

Melt the butter and olive oil in a pan and cook the onion and garlic; add the sultanas, break up and add the vermicelli. Add the rice and over a low flame continue to stir.

2

Pour in the stock, season it, bring to a boil and let it simmer on top of the stove 40 minutes.

3

Let the pilav stand 10 minutes uncovered, then stir with a fork to let in air.

MILLET PILAV

Egypt

Imperial (Metric)	American
4 tablespoons olive oil	4 tablespoons olive oil
½ lb (225g) millet	1 cup millet
3 crushed cloves garlic	3 crushed cloves garlic
sea salt and black pepper	sea salt and black pepper
8 fl oz (225ml) vegetable stock	1 cup vegetable stock
2 green peppers, finely chopped	2 green peppers, finely chopped
3 tomatoes, finely chopped	3 tomatoes, finely chopped
2 onions, finely chopped	2 onions, finely chopped
2 tablespoons each of parsley and mint, finely chopped	2 tablespoons each of parsley and mint; finely chopped

1

Heat the oil in a pan and add the millet, garlic and seasoning. Stir until the millet turns golden brown, then add the stock and simmer, covered, about 15 minutes.

2

Take the lid off and add the peppers, tomatoes and onions; stir and let cook another 2 minutes. Sprinkle the chopped herbs on just before serving.

BULGUR PILAV

Turkey

Imperial (Metric)	American
2 oz (55g) butter	$\frac{1}{4}$ cup butter
4 tablespoons olive oil	4 tablespoons olive oil
2 onions, finely chopped	2 onions, finely chopped
3 crushed cloves garlic	3 crushed cloves garlic
$\frac{1}{2}$ lb (225g) bulgur wheat	1 cup bulgur wheat
$\frac{3}{4}$ pint (425ml) vegetable stock	2 cups vegetable stock
sea salt and black pepper	sea salt and black pepper

1
Melt the butter with the oil in a pan and sauté the onion and garlic a few moments. Add the bulgur and continue to cook a few moments more.

2
Pour in the stock, bring to a boil and continue to cook a further 10 to 15 minutes. Check for seasoning before serving and add more butter if desired.

TAYIATELA ME MELITZANES
Tagliatelle with Aubergines (Eggplants)

Greece

Imperial (Metric)	American
2 aubergines	2 eggplants
¾ lb (340g) wholemeal tagliatelle	6–8 cups whole wheat tagliatelle
½ pint (285ml) tomato sauce	1¼ cups tomato sauce
(see page 104)	(see page 104)
4 oz (100g) Feta cheese, grated	1 cup grated Feta cheese
4 oz (100g) Gruyère cheese, grated	1 cup grated Gruyère cheese
3 oz (85g) butter	⅓ cup butter
5 tablespoons olive oil	5 tablespoons olive oil
sea salt and black pepper	sea salt and black pepper

1
Slice the aubergines (eggplant) and sprinkle salt over them. Leave an hour then wash the salt off and pat dry. Sauté them in butter and olive oil until just brown and crisp.

2
Meanwhile boil the tagliatelle in plenty of salted water about 20 minutes or until al dente. Drain carefully.

3
Butter a shallow fireproof dish and lay half the tagliatelle at the bottom of it. Cover with half the aubergine slices, then pour half the tomato sauce over the top. Sprinkle with half of each of the two cheeses then add a final layer of pasta, aubergine (eggplant), sauce and cheese.

4
Bake in a preheated 400°F/200°C (Gas Mark 6) oven 15 to 20 minutes or until the top is brown and bubbling.

KROKETES ME RYZI

Rice Croquettes

Greece

Imperial (Metric)	American
¾ lb (340g) brown rice	1½ cups brown rice
4 oz (100g) Feta cheese	1 cup Feta cheese
2 oz (55g) pine nuts	⅔ cup pine nuts
2 teaspoons dried oregano	2 teaspoons dried oregano
5 crushed cloves garlic	5 crushed cloves garlic
1 onion, finely chopped	1 onion, finely chopped
3 eggs	3 eggs
2 tablespoons parsley, finely chopped	2 tablespoons parsley, finely chopped
sea salt and black pepper	sea salt and black pepper
2 oz (55g) wholemeal flour	½ cup whole wheat flour
2 oz (55g) wholemeal breadcrumbs	1 cup fresh whole wheat breadcrumbs
corn oil for frying	corn oil for frying

1

Cook the rice in 1½ pints (850ml) water. When the rice is done add the cheese, nuts and oregano, garlic and onion to the pan. Stir well and mix thoroughly.

2

Separate the eggs and add the yolks to the rice. Add the parsley and seasoning and form into small cakes the size of a golf ball.

3

Roll them in flour, then egg white, then breadcrumbs and fry them in corn oil until crisp and brown.

RISI E BISI

Italy

Imperial (Metric)	American
2 lb (900g) peas in their pods	2 pounds peas in their pods
4 small artichokes	4 small artichokes
1 small onion, chopped	1 small onion, chopped
2 crushed cloves garlic	2 crushed cloves garlic
4 oz (100g) butter	$\frac{1}{2}$ cup butter
$\frac{1}{2}$ lb (225g) brown rice	1 cup brown rice
1$\frac{1}{2}$ pints (850ml) vegetable stock	3$\frac{3}{4}$ cups vegetable stock
sea salt and black pepper	sea salt and black pepper
2 oz (55g) grated Parmesan	$\frac{1}{2}$ cup grated Parmesan

1

Shell the peas, trim and quarter the young artichokes. Melt the butter in a large pan and cook the onion and garlic a moment or two. Add the vegetables to the butter, stir and cook a few moments more over moderate heat.

2

Add the rice and cook another 2 or 3 minutes, allowing the grains to absorb the butter. Pour in the stock, season and cook in a covered pan about 40 minutes. Stir in the grated Parmesan before serving.

FRIED POLENTA

Italy

Imperial (Metric)	American
½ lb (225g) cornmeal	1½ cups cornmeal
½ tablespoon salt	½ tablespoon salt
2½ pints (1.2 litres) water	6⅓ cups water
1 oz (30g) butter	2½ tablespoons butter
3 tablespoons olive oil	3 tablespoons olive oil

1

Boil the water with the salt and trickle in the cornmeal, stirring vigorously all the time. Let it simmer and continue to stir 10 minutes.

2

Turn the heat down low and leave on a heat diffuser; leave to cook gently 30 minutes. Pour out into a shallow earthenware dish or a baking tray and let set overnight.

3

Cut into small squares about 2 inches (5cm) and sauté in butter and oil until brown.

GNOCCHI ALLA ROMANA

Italy

Imperial (Metric)	American
1 pint (570ml) milk	2½ cups milk
sea salt and black pepper	sea salt and black pepper
½ teaspoon ground nutmeg	½ teaspoon ground nutmeg
6 oz (170g) wholemeal semolina	1½ cups whole wheat semolina
1 egg, beaten	1 egg, beaten
4 oz (100g) grated Parmesan	1 cup grated Parmesan
2 oz (55g) grated Gruyère	½ cup grated Gruyère
4 oz (100g) butter	½ cup butter

1

Add the nutmeg, salt and pepper to the milk, bring to a boil and pour in the semolina. Stir continuously over very low heat until it becomes a thick paste. Take away from the heat and allow to cool slightly.

2

Stir in the egg, add the Gruyère and half of the Parmesan and butter. Check for seasoning — it may need more black pepper.

3

Spread the paste on a dish or board and smooth it down to about ½ inch (1.25cm) thick and leave to cool (overnight if you wish).

4

Cut the mixture into squares or triangles and place in a shallow fireproof dish so that the pieces overlap. Pour the remaining butter over it and sprinkle with rest of the Parmesan cheese. Bake in a preheated 400°F/200°C (Gas Mark 6) oven about 20 minutes.

CANNELLONI STUFFED WITH CABBAGE PURÉE

Egypt

Imperial (Metric)	American
6 wholemeal cannelloni sheets	6 whole wheat cannelloni sheets
1 spring cabbage	1 spring cabbage
2 oz (55g) butter	¼ cup butter
1 teaspoon crushed coriander	1 teaspoon crushed coriander
2 oz (55g) Feta or salty goat cheese	2 ounces Feta or salty goat cheese
2 oz (55g) curd cheese	2 ounces cottage cheese
sea salt and black pepper	sea salt and black pepper
5 fl oz (150ml) sour cream	⅔ cup sour cream
2 tablespoons grated Parmesan	2 tablespoons grated Parmesan

1

Cook the cannelloni in plenty of boiling salted water 10 to 15 minutes or until the sheets are al dente. Leave to drain.

2

Slice the cabbage thinly and cook it in the butter with the coriander in a pan with a tightly fitting lid 10 minutes or until soft. Leave to cool, then place in a blender to purée. Mix in the Feta and curd (cottage) cheese and seasoning.

3

Place about 2 tablespoons of the mixture onto each sheet of cannelloni and roll, sealing each end. Place them on a buttered fireproof dish and cover with the sour cream; sprinkle with the Parmesan and bake in a preheated 400°F/200°C (Gas Mark 6) oven 15 to 20 minutes.

CANNELLONI STUFFED WITH LENTIL PURÉE

Tunisia

Imperial (Metric)	American
6 sheets wholemeal cannelloni	6 sheets whole wheat cannelloni
$\frac{1}{2}$ lb (225g) orange lentils	1 cup orange lentils
5 tablespoons olive oil	$\frac{1}{3}$ cup olive oil
5 crushed cloves garlic	5 crushed cloves garlic
1 onion	1 onion
1 teaspoon each oregano and cumin	1 teaspoon each oregano and cumin
1 green chilli chopped and seeded	1 green chili chopped and seeded
sea salt and black pepper	sea salt and black pepper
5 fl oz (150ml) sour cream	$\frac{2}{3}$ cup sour cream
2oz (55g) grated Parmesan	$\frac{1}{2}$ cup grated Parmesan

1

Cook the cannelloni in plenty of boiling water 10 to 15 minutes or until the sheets are al dente. Leave to drain. Soak the lentils $\frac{1}{2}$ hour. Pour the oil into a saucepan and add the garlic, onion, oregano, cumin and green chilli. Let cook 2 or 3 minutes.

2

Add the soaked lentils, let them cook a moment in the oil then add $1\frac{1}{2}$ pints (850ml) water and simmer 20 minutes. Let it cool then blend to a thick purée. If it is not thick enough add some breadcrumbs and curd (cottage) cheese. Season with salt and pepper.

3

Place about 2 tablespoons of the mixture onto each sheet of cannelloni and roll, sealing each end. Place them on a buttered fireproof dish and cover with the sour cream; sprinkle with the Parmesan and bake in a preheated 400°F/200°C (Gas Mark 6) oven 15 to 20 minutes.

POTATO GNOCCHI

Italy

Imperial (Metric)	American
1½ lb (680g) potatoes	1¼ pounds potatoes
4 oz (100g) wholemeal flour	1 cup whole wheat flour
2 oz (55g) butter	¼ cup butter
2 egg yolks	2 egg yolks
sea salt and black pepper	sea salt and black pepper

1

Peel and boil the potatoes. When they are done drain them well and place them back into the pan and over the heat again. Shake the pan vigorously so they are well dried out. Mash the potatoes and push them through a sieve.

2

Put the potatoes in a large mixing bowl and stir in the flour and butter; when it is thoroughly mixed stir in the egg yolks and season generously.

3

Roll out into a long sausage-shape and cut ¼-inch (6mm) slices from it. Have a pan of simmering salted water and drop the gnocchi into it. They are done after a few minutes; when they bob to the surface take them out with a slotted spoon and keep them warm. They are traditionally eaten with pesto and tomato sauce.

Chapter 7
Pies and Pizzas

TOURTE AUX FEUILLES DE BETTES
Swiss Chard Pie

France

Imperial (Metric)	American
For the pastry:	
10 oz (285g) wholemeal flour	2½ cups whole wheat flour
5 oz (140g) butter	⅔ cup butter
pinch of salt	pinch of salt
1 egg	1 egg
1 tablespoon of water	1 tablespoon of water
For the filling:	
2 lb (1.15kg) Swiss chard leaves	2 pounds Swiss chard leaves
2 tablespoons butter	2 tablespoons butter
6 oz (170g) curd cheese	¾ cupful fromage frais (low fat cream cheese)
2 oz (55g) grated Parmesan	½ cup grated Parmesan
3 crushed cloves garlic	3 crushed cloves garlic
sea salt and black pepper	sea salt and black pepper

Continued overpage

1

Make the pastry by sifting the flour into a bowl, add the salt and rub in the butter to make a texture like that of breadcrumbs. Beat the egg with the water and add to make a paste. Roll it out and cover the base and sides of a pie tin or pie plate.

2

Take the stalks from the Swiss chard leaves, slice them and steam them $\frac{1}{2}$ hour adding the chopped leaves after 20 minutes. Turn them into a mixing bowl and add the cheeses, garlic and seasoning.

3

Place this filling into the pie case and cover with pastry. Make a hole in the centre and glaze with a little beaten egg. Bake in a preheated 375°F/190°C (Gas Mark 5) oven $\frac{1}{2}$ hour.

TOURTIÈRE AUX SALSIFIS
Salsify Pie

France

Imperial (Metric)	*American*
(Pastry as for preceding recipe)	**(Pastry as for preceding recipe)**
1 14oz (400g) tin salsify	1 14-ounce can salsify
$\frac{1}{2}$ pint (285ml) tomato sauce	1$\frac{1}{3}$ cups tomato sauce
(see page 104)	(see page 104)
2 large onions, finely chopped	2 large onions, finely chopped
2 oz (55g) butter	$\frac{1}{4}$ cup butter
3 tablespoons chopped fresh	3 tablespoons chopped fresh
basil	basil
sea salt and black pepper	sea salt and black pepper
1 beaten egg	1 beaten egg

1

Make the pastry as above and line a pie tin or pie plate. Melt the butter in a pan and add the onion, cook until it is soft. Drain the salsify, add the salsify, and season well.

2

Pour the salsify and onion into the pie tin or pie plate. Beat the egg into the tomato sauce and add the basil. Pour this over the salsify and onion, place the pastry lid over the top and cook as for the preceding recipe.

TOURTIÈRE AUX CHAMPIGNONS
Mushroom Pie

France

Imperial (Metric) (Pastry as for preceding recipe)	American (Pastry as for preceding recipe)
½ lb (225g) mushrooms	4 cups mushrooms
6 oz (170g) cooked brown rice	¾ cup (raw) brown rice
2 onions, finely chopped	2 onions, finely chopped
2 oz (55g) butter	¼ cup butter
2 tablespoons chopped fresh sage	2 tablespoons chopped fresh sage
sea salt and black pepper	sea salt and black pepper
3 hard-boiled eggs	3 hard-cooked eggs
2 oz (55g) butter	¼ cup butter

1

Make the pastry as above and line a pie dish. Take the stalks from the mushrooms and place the mushrooms at the bottom of the dish, gill side up. Chop the stalks and place them on top of the mushrooms.

2

If rice is raw, cook it. Cook the onion in the butter until it is soft. Add the onion to the rice with the sage and seasoning and place on top of the mushrooms. Peel and halve the eggs and press these into the rice mixture. Melt the rest of the butter and pour this over the top. Cover with pastry and bake in a preheated 375°F/190°C (Gas Mark 5) oven ½ hour.

TYROPITTA
Cheese Pie

Greece

Imperial (Metric)	American
pinch of nutmeg	pinch of nutmeg
teaspoon black pepper	teaspoon black pepper
4 eggs	4 eggs
12 oz (340g) Feta cheese	1½ cups Feta cheese
½ lb (225g) cottage or curd cheese	1 cup cottage cheese
4 oz (100g) grated Parmesan	1 cup grated Parmesan
3 crushed cloves garlic	3 crushed cloves garlic
2 tablespoons finely chopped parsley	2 tablespoons finely chopped parsley
1 lb (450g) filo pastry	1 pound phyllo pastry
3 oz (85g) melted butter	⅓ cup melted butter

1
Add the nutmeg and pepper to the eggs and beat them with a fork. Crumble in the Feta cheese and stir in the other cheeses with the garlic and parsley.

2
Butter a wide but shallow metal pie dish and spread 7 or 8 layers of pastry in the following manner: Place the first one into the dish and paint it with melted butter, continue with the other layers always putting melted butter in between. Now put the cheese mixture over the last layer of pastry and cover with 4 or 6 layers more. Be generous with the melted butter on the last sheet for then the top will be crisp.

3
Bake in a preheated 375°F/190°C (Gas Mark 5) oven 40 minutes.

SPANAKOPITTA
Spinach Pie

Greece

Imperial (Metric)	American
2 lb (1.15kg) fresh spinach	2 pounds fresh spinach
1 onion, finely sliced	1 onion, finely chopped
1 bunch spring onions	1 bunch scallions
4 tablespoons olive oil	¼ cup olive oil
4 oz (100g) melted butter	½ cup melted butter
sea salt and black pepper	sea salt and black pepper
4 tablespoons finely chopped parsley	4 tablespoons finely chopped parsley
4 tablespoons chopped dill	4 tablespoons chopped dill
4 eggs	4 eggs
½ lb (225g) Feta cheese	1 cup Feta cheese
1 pound (450g) packet filo pastry	1 pound phyllo pastry

1

Chop the spinach and cook the onion and spring onions (scallions) in the olive oil; add the spinach and cook 4 or 5 minutes. Add the seasoning, parsley and dill and leave aside to cool. Drain off any excess liquid. Break the eggs into a mixing bowl, beat them with a fork and crumble in the Feta. Add the spinach and mix well.

2

Line a shallow but wide pie tin with 7 or 8 layers of pastry and melted butter as in the preceding recipe. Place the filling on the bottom and cover with 5 or 6 layers of pastry. Bake in a preheated 375°F/190°C (Gas Mark 5) oven 40 minutes.

PITTA BREAD

Lebanon

Imperial (Metric)	American
1 teaspoon dried yeast	1 teaspoon dried yeast
1 teaspoon brown sugar	1 teaspoon brown sugar
2 fl oz (60ml) warm water	$\frac{1}{4}$ cup warm water
$\frac{1}{2}$ lb (225g) strong white flour	2 cups white flour
$\frac{1}{2}$ lb (225g) wholemeal flour	2 cups whole wheat flour
$\frac{1}{2}$ teaspoon salt	$\frac{1}{2}$ teaspoon salt
10 oz (285ml) water	$1\frac{1}{3}$ cups water

1

Sprinkle the sugar onto the yeast and add the warm water. Leave it in a warm place about 20 minutes to start the yeast working.

2

In a large mixing bowl add the salt to the 2 flours and pour in the yeast. Make a dough and knead it on a board up to 15 minutes. Return it to the bowl and leave it, covered, in a warm place until doubled in size. Knead it again 2 or 3 minutes and then take off golf-ball-sized lumps; roll these out into circles about $\frac{1}{4}$ inch (6mm) deep and 5 inches (12cm) wide. Leave these in a warm place 20 minutes.

3

Preheat the oven to 450°F/230°C (Gas Mark 8) and place the dough on hot baking sheets in the oven 8 minutes. When they are done they can be slit in the middle and filled with various stuffings. They are in fact the most basic pie and can be eaten on the move.

LENTEN PIES

Egypt

Imperial (Metric)	American
(Pitta dough as for preceding recipe)	(Pitta dough as for preceding recipe)
4 oz (100g) sesame seeds	½ cup sesame seeds
2 oz (55g) cumin seeds	¼ cup cumin seeds
2 oz (55g) chopped almonds	½ cup chopped almonds
4 oz (100g) raw cane sugar	⅔ cup raw cane sugar
2 tablespoons corn oil	2 tablespoons corn oil

1

Have the pitta bread circles of dough ready to go into the oven. Combine all the other ingredients (you might need more oil to hold the mixture together).

2

Place about 2 tablespoons of the mixture onto each piece of dough. Bake in a preheated 400°F/200°C (Gas Mark 6) oven for 10 minutes.

CHICKPEA (GARBANZO) PIE

Turkey

Imperial (Metric)	American
½ lb (225g) cooked chickpeas	1 cup cooked garbanzos
3 crushed cloves garlic	3 crushed cloves garlic
2 oz (55g) sesame seeds	¼ cup sesame seeds
sea salt and black pepper	sea salt and black pepper

1

Prepare the pitta bread dough in their circles to go into the oven.

2

Mix the garlic with the chickpeas (garbanzos), press some of this mixture onto each circle, sprinkle with sesame seeds and season. Place in a preheated 400°F/200°C (Gas Mark 6) oven and bake for 10 minutes.

POTATO BOREKS

Turkey

Imperial (Metric)	American
1 lb (450g) potatoes	1 pound potatoes
2 tablespoons milk	2 tablespoons milk
3 oz butter	$\frac{1}{3}$ cup butter
1 egg, beaten	1 egg, beaten
2 tablespoons chopped parsley	2 tablespoons chopped parsley
2 tablespoons chopped mint	2 tablespoons chopped mint
sea salt and black pepper	sea salt and black pepper
2 sheets filo pastry	2 sheets phyllo pastry
2 oz (55g) melted butter	$\frac{1}{4}$ cup melted butter

1

Peel and quarter the potatoes and boil them until tender. Drain them well, place in a mixing bowl, add the milk, butter, beaten egg, parsley and mint, mix into a thick paste and add the sea salt and black pepper.

2

Cut each sheet of pastry into 4 and brush each with melted butter. Divide the potato purée into 8 and roll it into small sausage shapes. Place each one onto a piece of pastry and roll it up, tucking in the ends. Brush each one with melted butter.

3

Lay on an oiled baking sheet and place in a pre heated 375°F/190°C (Gas Mark 5) oven 25 minutes.

AUBERGINE (EGGPLANT) PIE

Malta

Imperial (Metric)	American
Shortcrust pastry made from wholemeal flour (see page 196)	Shortcrust pastry made from whole wheat flour (see page 196)
2 aubergines	2 eggplants
6 oz (170g) curd cheese	$\frac{2}{3}$ cup cottage cheese
2 oz hard salty cheese or Parmesan	$\frac{1}{2}$ cup hard salty cheese or Parmesan
$\frac{1}{4}$ pint (150ml) olive oil	$\frac{2}{3}$ cup olive oil
1 teaspoon oregano	1 teaspoon oregano
1 teaspoon thyme	1 teaspoon thyme
3 crushed cloves garlic	3 crushed cloves garlic
2 onions, chopped	2 onions, chopped
sea salt and black pepper	sea salt and black pepper
$\frac{1}{2}$ pint tomato sauce (see page 104)	$1\frac{1}{3}$ cups tomato sauce (see page 104)

1

Slice the aubergines (eggplants) across into $\frac{1}{4}$-inch (6mm) circles, sprinkle salt over them and leave 1 hour to lose some of their bitterness. Roll out half the pastry and line a pie dish with it. Mix the 2 cheeses and place on the pastry. Wash the salt off the aubergine (eggplant) slices and pat them dry.

2

Heat the olive oil and add the oregano, thyme and garlic, then the onions and the aubergine (eggplant) slices. Sauté until crisp.

3

Lay the aubergine (eggplant) and onion on top of the cheese, season with salt and pepper and cover with tomato sauce. Roll out the remaining pastry and place on top of the pie. Bake in a preheated 375°F/190°C (Gas Mark 5) oven 25 minutes.

TORTA DI ZUCCHINI
Courgette (Zucchini) Pie

Italy

Imperial (Metric)	American
1 lb (450g) shortcrust wholemeal pastry	1 lb (450g) shortcrust whole wheat pastry
2 lb (900g) courgettes	2 pounds zucchini
2 oz (55g) butter	¼ cup butter
sea salt and black pepper	sea salt and black pepper

For the sauce:

Imperial (Metric)	American
1 oz (30g) flour	¼ cup flour
1 oz (30g) butter	2½ tablespoons butter
5 fl oz (150ml) milk	⅔ cup milk
½ pint (285ml) single cream	1⅓ cups light cream
3 oz (85g) grated Parmesan	¾ cup grated Parmesan
2 egg yolks	2 egg yolks
sea salt and black pepper	sea salt and black pepper
pinch of nutmeg	pinch of nutmeg

1
Line a pie dish with half the pastry. Slice the courgettes (zucchini) into rounds and sauté them in the butter with the seasoning about 10 mintues or until soft.

2
Make the sauce by melting the butter, adding the flour and cooking it a moment; add the milk and then the cream and cheese. Have the egg yolks in a small mixing bowl and add a little of the sauce to them and then add the entire mixture to the pie. Season with salt, pepper and nutmeg. Now add the courgettes (zucchini) to the sauce and mix thoroughly. Pour it into the pie dish and roll out the pastry cover.

3
Bake in a preheated 375°F/190°C (Gas Mark 5) oven 25 minutes.

EMPANADA DE ALCACHOFAS CON VINO BLANCO

Pie of Artichokes in White Wine Sauce

Spain

Imperial (Metric)	American
1 lb (450g) wholemeal shortcrust pastry (see page 196)	1 lb (450g) whole wheat shortcrust pastry (see page 196)
12 baby artichokes or 14 oz (400g) tin of artichoke hearts	12 baby artichokes or 14-ounce can of artichoke hearts
2 onions, finely sliced	2 onions, finely sliced
3 crushed cloves garlic	3 crushed cloves garlic
1 tablespoon wholemeal flour	1 tablespoon whole wheat flour
5 fl oz (150ml) white wine	⅔ cup white wine
½ pint (285ml) strong celery stock	1⅓ cups strong celery stock
2 tablespoons chopped parsley	2 tablespoons chopped parsley

1

Line a pie dish with half of the pastry. If the artichokes are fresh, trim off stalks and outside leaves. Slice artichokes into quarters. Boil them 10 minutes, drain well and place them at the bottom of the pie. If using preserved artichoke hearts, drain the contents and place them at the bottom of the pie.

2

Heat the oil in a pan and cook the onions and garlic. When they are soft work in the flour and make a paste; work at that for a moment then add the celery stock and wine to make a fairly thick sauce. Add the seasoning and parsley and pour over the artichokes in the pie.

3

Roll out a piece of pastry to cover the pie and bake in a preheated 375°F/190°C (Gas Mark 5) oven 25 minutes.

PIZZA DOUGH

Italy

Imperial (Metric)	American
1½ teaspoons dried yeast	1½ teaspoons dried yeast
½ teaspoon sugar	½ teaspoon sugar
7 oz (200g) wholemeal flour	1¾ cups whole wheat flour
1 teaspoon salt	1 teaspoon salt
1 tablespoon olive oil	1 tablespoon olive oil

1

Mix the yeast with the sugar and 4 fl oz (100ml) warm water and leave in a warm place 15 minutes while the yeast does its work.

2

Sift the flour and add the salt. Pour the yeast and the oil into it and mix it into a smooth ball. Knead the dough 5 minutes. Place in a mixing bowl, cover with a damp cloth and leave in a warm place 2 hours or until it has doubled in bulk.

3

Roll out the dough to a large circle and then pinch the edges so that they are slightly risen; the sauce will now be spread on to the dough as in the following recipes.

PIZZA ALLA MARINARA
Pizza with Garlic and Tomatoes

Italy

Imperial (Metric)	American
½ pint (285ml) tomato sauce (see page 104)	1⅓ cups tomato sauce (see page 104)
5 garlic cloves, finely chopped	5 garlic cloves, finely chopped
2 teaspoons oregano	2 teaspoons oregano

1

Smear the tomato sauce liberally over the dough, sprinkle with the chopped garlic and the oregano. Bake in a preheated 425°F/220°C (Gas Mark 7) oven 20 minutes or until the edges of the pizza have risen and are brown.

Note

For Pizza Margherita, add slices of Mozzarella cheese and 1 oz (30g) grated Parmesan.

CALZONE
Folded-over Pizza

Italy

Imperial (Metric)	American
Pizza dough (see page 198)	Pizza dough (see page 198)
3 oz (85g) riccotta cheese	⅓ cup riccotta cheese
3 oz (85g) Mozzarella cheese, diced	⅓ cup Mozzarella cheese, diced
2 oz (55g) grated Parmesan	½ cup grated Parmesan
2 courgettes	2 zucchini
2 onions	2 onions
3 tablespoons olive oil	3 tablespoons olive oil
3 crushed cloves garlic	3 crushed cloves garlic
1 teaspoon oregano	1 teaspoon oregano
sea salt and black pepper	sea salt and black pepper

1
Mix all the cheeses together in a bowl. Slice the courgettes (zucchini) and onions and cook them in the oil with the garlic and oregano in a covered pan 10 minutes. When they are soft and cool add them to the cheeses and mix well.

2
Roll out the dough into a large circle, spoon the mixture onto half of the dough leaving a border of about ½ inch (1.25cm). Fold the dough over and seal the edges with your fingers. Brush some olive oil over the top of the calzone and bake in a preheated 450°F/230°C (Gas Mark 8) oven 15 minutes.

Chapter 8
Vegetable Dishes

PIMIENTOS RELLENOS
Stuffed Green Peppers

Spain

Imperial (Metric)	American
4 large green peppers	4 large green peppers
2 oz (55g) grated Manchego cheese	½ cup Manchego cheese, grated
2 oz (55g) grated Parmesan	2 oz (55g) grated Parmesan
4 tablespoons brown breadcrumbs	4 tablespoons brown breadcrumbs
12 black olives, stoned and chopped	12 black olives, pitted and chopped
2 crushed cloves garlic	2 crushed cloves garlic
sea salt and black pepper	sea salt and black pepper
2 tablespoons brandy	2 tablespoons brandy
5 fl oz (150ml) dry white wine	⅔ cup dry white wine

1
Slice the tops off the peppers and cut away the seeds and pith. Place peppers in a casserole dish with tightly fitting lid.

2
Mix all the remaining ingredients except for the wine. Stuff the peppers with the mixture, put the tops back onto the peppers, pour the wine over them, cover firmly and bake in a preheated 400°F/200°C (Gas Mark 6) oven 40 minutes.

CEBOLLAS RELLENOS
Stuffed Onions

Spain

Imperial (Metric)	American
4 large onions	4 large onions
4 tablespoons olive oil	4 tablespoons olive oil
4 crushed cloves garlic	4 crushed cloves garlic
1 green chilli cored, seeded and chopped	1 green chili cored, seeded and chopped
1 tablespoon ground fennel	1 tablespoon ground fennel
3 tomatoes, chopped	3 tomatoes, chopped
1 egg, beaten	1 egg, beaten
4 tablespoons wholemeal breadcrumbs	4 tablespoons whole wheat breadcrumbs
sea salt and black pepper	sea salt and black pepper

1

Peel onions and dig out a large central cavity. Boil the onion shells 4 to 5 minutes then drain. Cut up the rest of the onion and cook it in the olive oil with the garlic, chilli and fennel.

2

When the onion is soft, add the tomatoes and continue to cook another 4 minutes. Raise the heat to drive off any excess liquid and then pour into a bowl and let cool.

3

Add the egg and breadcrumbs to the mixture and season well. Stuff the central cavity of the onions and place them in an oiled fireproof dish and bake in a preheated 400°F/200°C (Gas Mark 6) oven 20 minutes.

POTAJE DE GARBANZOS
Chickpea (Garbanzo) Stew

Spain

Imperial (Metric)	American
1 lb (450g) chickpeas	2 cups garbanzos
3 slices wholemeal bread	3 slices whole wheat bread
3 crushed cloves garlic	3 crushed cloves garlic
5 fl oz (150ml) olive oil	⅔ cup olive oil
2 large onions	2 large onions
½ lb (225g) spinach leaves	½ pound spinach leaves
6 large tomatoes, peeled and chopped	6 large tomatoes, peeled and chopped
½ lb (225g) potatoes, peeled and diced	½ pound potatoes, peeled and diced
6 baby artichokes, trimmed and quartered	6 baby artichokes, trimmed and quartered
sea salt and black pepper	sea salt and black pepper
1 teaspoon ground cumin	1 teaspoon ground cumin
1 tablespoon oregano	1 tablespoon oregano
2 hard-boiled eggs, chopped fine	2 hard-cooked eggs, chopped fine
1 tablespoon chopped parsley	1 tablespoon chopped parsley

1
Soak the chickpeas overnight. Boil them in salted water 2 hours.

2
Sauté the bread and the garlic with a little of the olive oil and reserve.
Pour the rest of the olive oil into a pan and add the onions; sauté until
soft, then add the spinach leaves and tomatoes and continue to cook
another 20 minutes.

3
Half an hour before the chickpeas (garbanzos) are done add the potatoes
and artichokes. Mash the fried bread and garlic to the consistency of bread
sauce. Now add the chickpeas (garbanzos), potatoes and artichokes to the
onion and spinach with enough of the stock to make a thick stew. Stir in
the bread mash. Season to taste with salt, pepper, cumin and oregano.

4
Before serving, sprinkle on the chopped hard-boiled egg and finally the
parsley.

MENESTRA DE VERDURAS
Mixed Vegetables

Spain

Imperial (Metric)	American
6 small artichokes	6 small artichokes
10 asparagus spears	10 asparagus spears
½ lb (225g) green beans	½ pound green beans
½ lb (225g) shelled peas	1⅓ cups shelled peas
½ lb (225g) carrots	½ pound carrots
1 head of celery	1 head of celery
½ lb (225g) mushrooms	4 cups mushrooms
5 fl oz (150ml) olive oil	⅔ cup olive oil
1 pint (570ml) vegetable stock	2½ cups vegetable stock
sea salt and black pepper	sea salt and black pepper

For the sauce:

Imperial (Metric)	American
3 tablespoons olive oil	3 tablespoons olive oil
2 chopped onions	2 chopped onions
5 crushed cloves garlic	5 crushed cloves garlic
1 teaspoon oregano	1 teaspoon oregano
2 large tomatoes, peeled and chopped	2 large tomatoes, peeled and chopped
sea salt and black pepper	sea salt and black pepper

1
Trim and quarter the artichokes and chop the rest of the vegetables small. In a large casserole pour in the olive oil and add all the vegetables. Let them sauté in the oil 3–4 minutes then add the hot stock and seasoning. Place in a preheated 350°F/180°C (Gas Mark 4) oven about 1 hour.

2
Before the vegetables are cooked through, make the sauce. Heat the oil and add the onion, garlic and oregano. Cook until soft, add the chopped tomatoes and seasoning and cook a further 5 minutes.

3
Pour the sauce over the vegetables before serving.

PATITAS EN MOJO
New Potatoes with Chilli Sauce

Spain

Imperial (Metric)	American
1 lb (450g) new potatoes	1 pound new potatoes
2 dried red chillis	2 dried red chilis
½ teaspoon cumin seeds	½ teaspoon cumin seeds
3 crushed cloves garlic	3 crushed cloves garlic
1 tablespoon paprika	1 tablespoon paprika
sea salt	sea salt
2 tablespoons red wine vinegar	2 tablespoons red wine vinegar
½ pint (150ml) olive oil	⅔ cup olive oil

1
Steam the potatoes in their skins. Before they are cooked through make the sauce, either in a mortar or an electric blender.

2
Crush to a powder the red chillis and cumin seeds, and add the garlic, paprika and salt. Pour the vinegar in slowly then add the olive oil to make an emulsion.

3
Serve the potatoes hot with the sauce in a separate dish.

POMMES DE TERRE EN MATELOTE

France

Imperial (Metric)	American
1 lb (450g) boiled potatoes	1 pound boiled potatoes
2 oz (55g) butter	¼ cup butter
2 tablespoons each parsley and chives	2 tablespoons each parsley and chives
sea salt and black pepper	sea salt and black pepper
½ pint (285ml) vegetable stock	1⅓ cups vegetable stock
5 fl oz (150ml) dry white wine	⅔ cup dry white wine
2 egg yolks	2 egg yolks

1

Have a large casserole dish and cut the boiled potatoes in half. Place them in a dish with the butter, herbs and seasoning. Pour in the stock and the wine.

2

Cook on top of the stove about 10 minutes and then thicken the sauce with the egg yolks, as follows. Add a little stock to the egg yolks in a bowl, stir together and then return the contents of the bowl to the casserole.

POMMES DE TERRE À LA MANIÈRE D'APT

France

Imperial (Metric)	American
1 lb (450g) potatoes	1 pound potatoes
5 fl oz (150ml) olive oil	⅔ cup olive oil
4 tablespoons tomato purée	4 tablespoons tomato paste
2 bay leaves	2 bay leaves
sea salt and black pepper	sea salt and black pepper
½ pint (285ml) vegetable stock	1⅓ cups vegetable stock
6 stoned black olives	6 pitted black olives
3 tablespoons wholemeal breadcrumbs	3 tablespoons whole wheat breadcrumbs

1

Slice the potatoes into ¼-inch (6mm) rounds. In a shallow earthenware dish pour the olive oil and add the tomato purée, bay leaves and seasoning. Add the potatoes and cook about 5 minutes. Add the hot stock and simmer ½ hour.

2

Scatter the olives over the top, sprinkle with breadcrumbs and bake in a preheated 350°F/180°C (Gas Mark 4) oven 30 minutes.

POIREAUX À LA PROVENÇALE
Leeks Provençale

France

Imperial (Metric)	American
2 lb (900g) leeks	2 pound leeks
3 tablespoons olive oil	3 tablespoons olive oil
peel and juice of 1 lemon	peel and juice of 1 lemon
1 lb (450g) tomatoes, chopped	1 pound tomatoes, chopped
10 black olives stoned and halved	10 black olives pitted and halved
sea salt and black pepper	sea salt and black pepper

1

Clean and chop the leeks, pour the oil into an earthenware dish and simmer the leeks 5 minutes. Add the lemon juice, chopped peel, chopped tomatoes and the olives. Season, stir and leave to cook over a low flame another 10 minutes.

BEIGNETS D'AUBERGINES (EGGPLANTS)

France

Imperial (Metric)	American
2 aubergines	2 eggplants

For the batter:	
4 oz (100g) flour	1 cup flour
3 tablespoons olive oil	3 tablespoons olive oil
pinch of salt	pinch of salt
6 oz (180ml) water	$\frac{2}{3}$ cup water
1 egg white, beaten	1 egg white, beaten

1

Slice the aubergines (eggplant) across in $\frac{1}{4}$ inch (6mm) rounds, sprinkle salt on them and leave 1 hour.

2

Make the batter by mixing the flour and oil with the salt then adding the water gradually, beating all the time to keep the batter smooth. Fold in the egg white at the last moment.

3

Wash the salt from the aubergines (eggplant) and pat them dry. Dip them in the batter and fry in very hot corn oil.

RATATOUILLE

France

Imperial (Metric)	American
5 fl oz (150ml) olive oil	$\frac{2}{3}$ cup olive oil
1 tablespoon oregano	1 tablespoon oregano
2 large onions, chopped	2 large onions, chopped
2 large aubergines, sliced and salted 1 hour, washed and dried	2 large eggplants sliced and salted 1 hour, washed and dried
3 green peppers, cored and seeded	3 green peppers, cored and seeded
3 courgettes, sliced	3 zucchini, sliced
$\frac{1}{2}$ pint (285ml) tomato sauce (page 104)	$1\frac{1}{3}$ cups tomato sauce (page 104)
sea salt and black pepper	sea salt and black pepper

1

Pour the oil into a large shallow pan; add the oregano, then the onions, aubergines, (eggplant) peppers and courgettes (zucchini). Cover the pan and let simmer 30 minutes.

2

Add the tomato sauce and leave the pan uncovered to simmer a further 10 minutes.

CHAMPIGNONS À LA PROVENÇALE

France

Imperial (Metric)	American
½ lb (225g) mushrooms	4 cups mushrooms
4 tablespoons olive oil	4 tablespoons olive oil
3 crushed cloves garlic	3 crushed cloves garlic
sea salt and black pepper	sea salt and black pepper
3 tablespoons chopped parsley	3 tablespoons chopped parsley

1
Slice the mushrooms and cook them in the olive oil and garlic until just soft.

2
Season well and sprinkle in the parsley.

TOMATES PROVENÇALES

France

Imperial (Metric)	American
2 large tomatoes	2 large tomatoes
2 crushed cloves garlic	2 crushed cloves garlic
3 tablespoons wholemeal breadcrumbs	3 tablespoons whole wheat breadcrumbs
5 tablespoons chopped basil	5 tablespoons chopped basil
2 tablespoons olive oil	2 tablespoons olive oil
2 tablespoons grated Gruyère	2 tablespoons grated Gruyère
sea salt and black pepper	sea salt and black pepper

1

Slice the tomatoes in half and extract all of their pulp. Chop it quite small and place in a bowl. Add the rest of the ingredients.

2

Fill the tomato shells with stuffing and place under a very hot grill 5 minutes or until top is crisp and very slightly burnt.

CAPONATINA
Aubergines (Eggplants) in a Sweet-and-sour Sauce

Sicily

Imperial (Metric)	American
3 aubergines	3 eggplants
5 fl oz (150ml) olive oil	$\frac{2}{3}$ cup olive oil
1 onion sliced	1 onion sliced
$\frac{1}{2}$ pint (285ml) tomato sauce (page 104)	$1\frac{1}{3}$ cups tomato sauce (page 104)
2 oz (55g) capers	$\frac{1}{3}$ cup capers
2 oz (55g) green olives, stoned and halved	$\frac{1}{2}$ cup green olives, pitted and halved
1 tablespoon raw cane sugar	1 tablespoon raw cane sugar
2 tablespoons red wine vinegar	2 tablespoons red wine vinegar
2 oz (55g) sultanas	$\frac{1}{3}$ cup golden seedless raisins
2 oz (55g) pine nuts	$\frac{1}{3}$ cup pine nuts
sea salt and black pepper	sea salt and black pepper

1

Slice the aubergines (eggplants), sprinkle salt on them and leave 1 hour. Wash.

2

Heat the oil in a pan and sauté the aubergine (eggplant) slices. When they are crisp, take them out and lay them on a platter.

3

Cook the onion in the oil that is left, until soft, add the tomato sauce and then the rest of the ingredients. Cook 15 minutes then pour the sauce over the aubergines (eggplant) and place in a hot oven 10 minutes.

PASTICCIO DI PATATE
Baked Potato Purée

Italy

Imperial (Metric)	American
2¼ lb (1.38kg) potatoes	2½ pounds potatoes
5 fl oz (150ml) milk	⅔ cup milk
3 oz (85g) butter	⅓ cup butter
2 oz (55g) grated Parmesan	½ cup grated Parmesan
2 tablespoons chopped basil	2 tablespoons chopped basil
2 tablespoons chopped parsley	2 tablespoons chopped parsley
1 teaspoon grated lemon rind	1 teaspoon grated lemon rind
pinch of nutmeg	pinch of nutmeg
2 oz (55g) Mozzarella cheese, diced	½ cup Mozzarella cheese, diced
3 tablespoons wholemeal breadcrumbs	3 tablespoons whole wheat breadcrumbs

1
Peel the potatoes and boil them, drain them well and put them through a sieve.

2
Beat in the rest of the ingredients except for the breadcrumbs.

3
Butter a soufflé dish and pile the mixture in, sprinkle it with the breadcrumbs and bake in a preheated 375°F/190°C (Gas Mark 5) oven 20 minutes.

ROTOLO DI SPINACI
Spinach Roll

Italy

Imperial (Metric)	American
1 lb (450g) potatoes	1 pound potatoes
1 egg, beaten	1 egg, beaten
5 oz (140g) wholemeal flour	1¼ cups whole wheat flour
1 teaspoon baking powder	1 teaspoon baking powder
sea salt and black pepper	sea salt and black pepper
1 onion, chopped	1 onion, chopped
2 tablespoons olive oil	2 tablespoons olive oil
1½ lbs (680g) spinach, cooked and chopped	3 cups spinach, cooked and chopped
4 oz (100g) ricotta cheese	½ cup ricotta cheese
4 oz (100g) grated Parmesan	½ cup grated Parmesan
pinch of nutmeg	pinch of nutmeg
2 egg yolks	2 egg yolks
1 oz (30g) melted butter	2½ tablespoons melted butter
1 oz (30g) grated Parmesan	¼ cup grated Parmesan

1

Peel and boil the potatoes. When they are done, put them through a sieve. Add to the potatoes the beaten egg, flour and baking powder. Work it into a paste, adding some salt and pepper. Knead into a dough.

2

Cook the onion in the olive oil and add the spinach; let it cook a few moments then pour it into a mixing bowl and add the 2 cheeses, the nutmeg, egg yolks and seasoning. Mix thoroughly.

3

Roll out the potato dough into a rectangle about 12-by-15 inches (30×40cm). Spread the spinach mixture over it leaving a 1-inch (2.5cm) border all round. Roll into a sausage shape then wrap the roll in a muslin cloth, tie both ends and lower the roll into a pan of lightly boiling salted water. Simmer 30 minutes, take the roll out and let it rest and cool.

4

Unwrap the roll from its bag and slice it into ¾-inch (2cm) slices, place in an earthenware dish so that the slices overlap. Pour some melted butter over it and the remaining grated Parmesan and bake in a preheated 400°F/200°C (Gas Mark 6) oven 15 minutes.

LAHANORIZO
Cabbage and Rice Casserole

Greece

Imperial (Metric)	American
2 onions, finely sliced	2 onions, finely sliced
1 medium-sized white cabbage, cored and shredded	1 medium-sized white cabbage, cored and shredded
5 fl oz (150ml) olive oil	$\frac{2}{3}$ cup olive oil
4 oz (100g) cooked brown rice	$\frac{2}{3}$ cup cooked brown rice
2 tablespoons tomato purée	2 tablespoons tomato paste
juice and zest of 1 lemon	juice and zest of 1 lemon
sea salt and black pepper	sea salt and black pepper
1 tablespoon each chopped parsley and mint	1 tablespoon each chopped parsley and mint

1

Sauté the onion and cabbage in the olive oil 2 or 3 minutes then add the rice, tomato purée, lemon juice, zest and seasoning. Give it a good stir and simmer 10 minutes.

2

Take away from the heat and let rest 5 minutes, then pour into a serving bowl and add the herbs.

PRASSORIZO
Leeks with Rice

Greece

Imperial (Metric)	American
2 lb (900g) leeks	2 pounds leeks
2 onions, sliced	2 onions, sliced
5 fl oz (150ml) olive oil	⅔ cup olive oil
4 oz (100g) cooked brown rice	⅔ cup cooked brown rice
juice and zest of 2 lemons	juice and zest of 2 lemons
sea salt and black pepper	sea salt and black pepper
1 tablespoon chopped parsley	1 tablespoon chopped parsley

1

Trim, clean and slice the leeks, then cook them with the onion in the oil 2 or 3 minutes. Add the rest of the ingredients except the parsley, stir well and simmer 10 minutes.

2

Take away from the heat and let rest 5 minutes, then pour into a serving bowl and add the parsley.

PATATES LEMONATES
Potatoes in Lemon Sauce

Greece

Imperial (Metric)	American
2 lb (900g) potatoes	2 pounds potatoes
juice and zest of 2 lemons	juice and zest of 2 lemons
4 oz (100g) butter	½ cup butter
5 fl oz (150ml) water	⅔ cup water
sea salt and black pepper	sea salt and black pepper

1
Peel the potatoes and cut them into quarters, all roughly the same size — about 1½-inches (3.75cm) across. Butter a deep casserole, place the potatoes in it, pour the lemon juice and zest over them, then the water. Season and dot the butter over the top.

2
Bake in a preheated 375°F/190°C (Gas Mark 5) oven 1 hour.

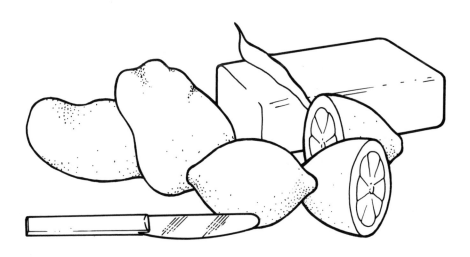

ARAKAS ME ANGINARES
Fresh Peas with Globe Artichokes

Greece

Imperial (Metric)	American
2 lb (900g) peas in their pods	2 pounds peas in their pods
6 young artichokes	6 young artichokes
5 fl oz (150ml) olive oil	$\frac{2}{3}$ cup olive oil
2 tablespoons dill	2 tablespoons dill
$\frac{3}{4}$ pint (425ml) water	2 cups water
juice and zest of 2 lemons	juice and zest of 2 lemons
sea salt and black pepper	sea salt and black pepper
1 bunch spring onions	1 bunch scallions

1
Shell the peas and trim and quarter the artichokes. Pour the oil into a pan with the dill and cook the peas and artichokes in it about 3 minutes, then add the water, lemons and seasoning.

2
Simmer gently 30 minutes giving the vegetables a stir every now and again. Chop the spring onions (scallions) and add them 5 minutes before the end of cooking.

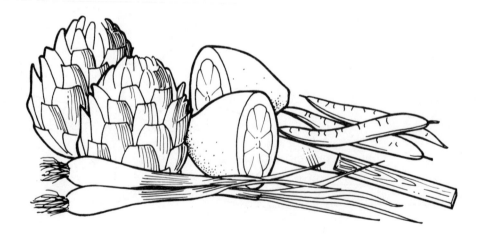

STUFFED PEPPERS

Italy

Imperial (Metric)	American
6 peppers	6 peppers
1 onion	1 onion
2 courgettes	2 zucchini
3 tablespoons olive oil	3 tablespoons olive oil
5 crushed cloves garlic	5 crushed cloves garlic
2 tablespoons capers	2 tablespoons capers
6 black olives, stoned and chopped	6 black olives, pitted and chopped
4 oz (100g) dried wholemeal breadcrumbs	1 cup dried whole wheat breadcrumbs
sea salt and black pepper	sea salt and black pepper
2 oz (55g) grated Parmesan	$\frac{1}{2}$ cup grated Parmesan
2 oz (55g) grated Gruyère	$\frac{1}{2}$ cup grated Gruyère
2 oz (55g) butter	$\frac{1}{4}$ cup butter
5 fl oz (150ml) celery stock	$\frac{2}{3}$ cup celery stock

1

Cut the tops from the peppers and reserve, seed and remove the rind from the peppers. Slice the onion and the courgettes (zucchini), cook in the olive oil until soft and add the garlic. Pour into a bowl and mix in the capers and olives, then the breadcrumbs, seasoning and cheeses.

2

Fill the peppers with this mixture. Fit them into a saucepan and put their tops back on.

3

Mix the butter with the stock and pour over the top. Place the saucepan over low heat so that it just simmers and leave to cook 30 to 40 minutes. Drain them well. Can be eaten hot, warm or cold.

PEPERONATA

Italy

Imperial (Metric)	American
2 lb (900g) red, green and yellow peppers	2 pounds red, green and yellow peppers
5 fl oz (150ml) olive oil	$\frac{2}{3}$ cup olive oil
2 large onions, sliced	2 large onions, sliced
5 crushed cloves garlic	5 crushed cloves garlic
sea salt and black pepper	sea salt and black pepper
1 lb (450g) tomatoes	1 pound tomatoes

1
Core and seed the peppers, slice them thinly. Pour the oil into a pan and cook the peppers, onions and garlic, with the seasoning, about 15 to 20 minutes.

2
Place the tomatoes in a covered pan and cook them about 10 minutes in their own juices over a low flame. Let them cool, then blend and sieve. Add the resulting tomato purée to the peppers and onion. Let that cook a further 10 minutes.

3
Pour into a bowl and cool. Serve with bread.

PEPPERONI IN TORTIERA

Italy

Imperial (Metric)	American
1 each green, yellow and red peppers	1 each green, yellow and red peppers
3 crushed cloves garlic	3 crushed cloves garlic
1 tablespoon each chopped mint and parsley	1 tablespoon each chopped mint and parsley
3 tablespoons wholemeal breadcrumbs	3 tablespoons whole wheat breadcrumbs
5 tablespoons olive oil	5 tablespoons olive oil
sea salt and black pepper	sea salt and black pepper
1 tablespoon lemon juice	1 tablespoon lemon juice
6 black olives, stoned and sliced	6 black olives, pitted and sliced

1

Burn and blister the peppers under a hot grill or over a flame. Scrape the skin away. Slice the flesh and discard the core. Lay the strips in a shallow dish.

2

Add the crushed garlic and herbs to the breadcrumbs with 2 tablespoons of oil, then the seasoning and lemon juice. Pour this over the peppers. Scatter the chopped olives over the top, pour the rest of the oil over that and bake in a 400°F/200°C (Gas Mark 6) oven about 10 to 12 minutes. Serve hot or warm.

SABBATH PEPPERS

Israel

Imperial (Metric)	American
4 large green peppers	4 large green peppers
4 oz (100g) walnuts, ground	1 cup ground walnuts
8 tablespoons matzo meal	8 tablespoons matzo meal
4 tablespoons wholemeal breadcrumbs	4 tablespoons whole wheat breadcrumbs
4 crushed cloves garlic	4 crushed cloves garlic
2 onions, finely sliced	2 onions, finely sliced
1 teaspoon dill	1 teaspoon dill
1 teaspoon fresh marjoram	1 teaspoon fresh marjoram
sea salt and black pepper	sea salt and black pepper
2 tablespoons olive oil	2 tablespoons olive oil

1

Slice the tops off the peppers and cut out all the pith and seeds. Pour the olive oil into a pan and cook the onion and garlic a few moments then add all the rest of the ingredients mixing well.

2

Stuff the peppers with the mixture, place the tops on each one and fit them snugly into a casserole dish. Pour a little water into the base of the dish and bake them in a preheated 375°F/190°C (Gas Mark 5) oven 40 to 45 minutes.

COURGETTES YAHNI

Greece

Imperial (Metric)	American
1 lb (450g) courgettes	1 pound zucchini
1 bunch spring onions	1 bunch scallions
4 tomatoes	4 tomatoes
2 crushed cloves garlic	2 crushed cloves garlic
$\frac{1}{2}$ teaspoon coriander, ground	$\frac{1}{2}$ teaspoon coriander, ground
$\frac{1}{2}$ teaspoon paprika	$\frac{1}{2}$ teaspoon paprika
4 tablespoons olive oil	4 tablespoons olive oil
sea salt and black pepper	sea salt and black pepper
juice of 1 lemon	juice of 1 lemon

1
Slice the courgettes (zucchini) lengthways into quarters, chop the spring onions (scallions), and peel and chop the tomatoes. Pour the oil in a pan and cook the spring onions (scallions), garlic and tomatoes a few moments, add the coriander and paprika, then lay the courgettes (zucchini) in the sauce, season and cover the pan and let simmer 25 minutes.

2
Before serving sprinkle with the lemon juice.

SESAME POTATOES

Greece

Imperial (Metric)	American
1 lb (450g) potatoes	1 pound potatoes
10 black olives, stoned and diced	10 black olives, pitted and diced
2 tablespoons freshly chopped basil	2 tablespoons freshly chopped basil
1 oz (30g) butter	$2\frac{1}{2}$ tablespoons butter
2 tablespoons matzo meal	2 tablespoons matzo meal
2 oz (55g) sesame seeds	$\frac{1}{4}$ cup sesame seeds
sea salt and black pepper	sea salt and black pepper

1
Peel and boil the potatoes. Mash them into a purée and put them in a mixing bowl.

2
Add the rest of the ingredients except the sesame seeds. Form into small cakes and roll them in the sesame seeds.

3
Sauté them until they are brown and crisp.

BAMIES
Casseroled Okra

Greece

Imperial (Metric)	American
1 lb (450g) fresh okra	1 pound fresh okra
1 large onion, sliced	1 large onion, sliced
5 fl oz (150ml) olive oil	$\frac{2}{3}$ cup olive oil
1 lb (450g) fresh tomatoes, skinned and chopped	1 pound fresh tomatoes, skinned and chopped
2 tablespoons chopped parsley	2 tablespoons chopped parsley
sea salt and black pepper	sea salt and black pepper

1

Trim the okra by the merest top and tailing; if you take off too much of the top you will lose the juices. Pour the oil into a pan, add the onion, tomatoes and seasoning; allow it to cook a few minutes then throw in the okra and stir into the sauce. Add the parsley and put the lid on the casserole and bake in a preheated 350°F/180°C (Gas Mark 4) oven 45 minutes.

SPANAKI ME LEMONI

Spinach Cooked with Lemon

Greece

Imperial (Metric)	American
2 lb (900g) fresh spinach	2 pounds fresh spinach
2 oz (55g) butter	$\frac{1}{4}$ cup butter
1 large onion, sliced	1 large onion, sliced
sea salt and black pepper	sea salt and black pepper
juice and zest of 1 lemon	juice and zest of 1 lemon

1

Wash and chop the spinach leaves, melt the butter in a pan and add the onions. Cook a moment then add the spinach. Season, cover the pan and simmer 10 minutes.

2

Take the lid off the pan and pour in the lemon juice and zest. Raise the heat, stir and let the spinach cook a few moments more while the excess moisture is driven off.

KOUNOUPITHI KAPAMA
Cauliflower Casserole

Greece

Imperial (Metric)	American
1 large cauliflower	1 large cauliflower
2 oz (55g) butter	$\frac{1}{4}$ cup butter
1 onion, sliced	1 onion, sliced
2 crushed cloves garlic	2 crushed cloves garlic
juice and zest of 1 lemon	juice and zest of 1 lemon
5 fl oz (150ml) water	$\frac{2}{3}$ cup water
3 tablespoons tomato purée	3 tablespoons tomato paste
sea salt and black pepper	sea salt and black pepper
2 tablespoons chopped parsley	2 tablespoons chopped parsley

1

Slice the cauliflower into its individual florets, melt the butter in a casserole dish and cook the onion and garlic until soft. Add the lemon juice, water and tomato purée and make a sauce. Season with salt and pepper then add the cauliflower, spooning the sauce over each piece.

2

Place the lid on the casserole dish and simmer about 10 minutes. Sprinkle the parsley over the dish and serve.

CATALAN SPINACH

Spain

Imperial (Metric)	American
2 lb (900g) spinach	2 pounds spinach
3 tablespoons olive oil	3 tablespoons olive oil
3 crushed cloves garlic	3 crushed cloves garlic
3 tablespoons pine nuts	3 tablespoons pine nuts
3 tablespoons currants	3 tablespoons currants
sea salt and black pepper	sea salt and black pepper

1

Wash and chop the spinach and place in a saucepan; cover and cook over low heat 10–12 minutes or until the spinach has lost its bulk by two-thirds. Let it cool, then drain and place in a blender and reduce to a thick purée. Place in a fireproof dish in a warm oven.

2

Cook the garlic in the olive oil and add the pine nuts and currants; stir and cook a few moments. Add salt and pepper and pour over the spinach.

3

Raise the oven temperature so the spinach reheats.

SPICED CAULIFLOWER

Lebanon

Imperial (Metric)	American
1 large cauliflower	1 large cauliflower
1 lb (450g) sweet red peppers	1 pound sweet red peppers
4 oz (100g) fresh red chillies	4 ounces fresh red chilis
5 fl oz (150ml) olive oil	$\frac{2}{3}$ cup olive oil
juice and zest of 1 lemon	juice and zest of 1 lemon
sea salt	sea salt

1

Slice the cauliflower into individual florets and boil in a little salted water about 5 minutes, drain well and reserve.

2

Slice and seed the peppers and chillies, boil them until tender, (about 8 minutes) then drain and place in a blender. Blend to a purée, adding the olive oil, lemon juice and salt.

3

Place the cauliflower in a warm serving dish and pour the hot sauce over the top.

VEGETABLE CASSEROLE I

Tunisia

Imperial (Metric)	American
5 fl oz (150ml) olive oil	⅔ cup olive oil
6 cloves garlic	6 cloves garlic
2 carrots, sliced	2 carrots, sliced
2 onions, sliced	2 onions, sliced
4 potatoes, peeled and cubed	4 potatoes, peeled and cubed
2 courgettes, sliced	2 zucchini, sliced
1 aubergine, cubed	1 eggplant, cubed
2 hot chilli peppers, seeded and chopped	2 hot chili peppers, seeded and chopped
1 teaspoon ground cumin	1 teaspoon ground cumin
1 teaspoon ground coriander	1 teaspoon ground coriander
2 tablespoons chopped parsley	2 tablespoons chopped parsley
5 fl oz (150ml) yogurt	⅔ cup yogurt
sea salt and black pepper	sea salt and black pepper

1

Pour the oil into a large casserole and add all the vegetables and spices. Let it cook 3–4 minutes, stirring all the time so the vegetables are covered in the oil.

2

Add enough boiling water to just cover the vegetables. Bring it to a boil, cover and bake in a preheated 350°F/180°C (Gas Mark 4) oven 45 minutes. Take from the oven and stir in the yogurt and parsley.

VEGETABLE CASSEROLE II

Turkey

Imperial (Metric)	American
2 green peppers	2 green peppers
2 red peppers	2 red peppers
6 cloves garlic	6 cloves garlic
2 courgettes	2 zucchini
1 aubergine	1 eggplant
5 fl oz (150ml) olive oil	$\frac{2}{3}$ cup olive oil
1 lb (450g) tomatoes, peeled and chopped	1 pound tomatoes, peeled and chopped
sea salt and black pepper	sea salt and black pepper
$\frac{1}{2}$ pint (285ml) yogurt	$1\frac{1}{3}$ cups yogurt

1

Core and seed all the peppers, peel the garlic, slice the courgettes (zucchini) and cube the aubergine (eggplant). Pour the oil into a casserole and add these vegetables. Let it cook 4–5 minutes.

2

Add the tomatoes, the seasoning and enough water just to cover the top of the vegetables.

3

Place in a preheated 350°F/180°C (Gas Mark 4) oven 45 minutes. Stir in the yogurt just before serving.

HARICOTS VERTS À LA PROVENÇALE

France

Imperial (Metric)	American
1 lb (450g) French beans	1 pound green beans
3 tablespoons olive oil	3 tablespoons olive oil
2 crushed cloves garlic	2 crushed cloves garlic
3 tomatoes, peeled and chopped	3 tomatoes, peeled and chopped
2 tablespoons chopped parsley	2 tablespoons chopped parsley
sea salt and black pepper	sea salt and black pepper

1
Trim the beans and slice them into 1-inch (2.5cm) lengths. Boil them in a little salted water 5 minutes; drain well.

2
Meanwhile cook the garlic in the oil and add the tomatoes. Let them bubble away so that the tomato cooks to a purée.

3
Tip the beans into a warm serving dish, pour the sauce over them and sprinkle with parsley.

FINOCCHIO ALLA PARMIGIANA
Fennel with Parmesan Cheese

Italy

Imperial (Metric)	American
6 heads fennel	6 heads fennel
2 oz (55g) butter	¼ cup butter
4 tablespoons grated Parmesan	4 tablespoons grated Parmesan
sea salt and black pepper	sea salt and black pepper

1

Trim and halve the fennel. Boil them in salted water 8–10 minutes. Drain them well then liberally butter a shallow fireproof dish. Lay the fennel into this and sprinkle with a lot of black pepper. Cover with the Parmesan cheese and the rest of the butter.

2

Place in a preheated 400°F/200°C (Gas Mark 6) oven 15 minutes or until the butter is bubbling and the cheese is golden brown.

FENOUIL À LA NIÇOISE

France

Imperial (Metric)	American
6 fennel halved	6 fennel, halved
2 onions, chopped	2 onions, chopped
3 crushed cloves garlic	3 crushed cloves garlic
2 tablespoons olive oil	2 tablespoons olive oil
½ pint (285ml) tomato sauce (see page 104)	1⅓ cups tomato sauce (see page 104)
6 black olives stoned and chopped	6 black olives, pitted and chopped
3 oz (85g) grated Gruyère	¾ cup grated Gruyère

1

Cook the fennel in boiling water 8–10 minutes. Drain well, then reserve.

2

Cook the onions and garlic in the olive oil until they are soft, add the tomato sauce and the olives.

3

Place the fennel in a fireproof dish and pour the sauce over them. Sprinkle the Gruyère cheese over the top and bake in a preheated 400°F/200°C (Gas Mark 6) oven for 10 minutes.

PROVENÇALE TIAN

France

Imperial (Metric)	American
6 large onions	6 large onions
2 tablespoons olive oil	2 tablespoons olive oil
2 crushed cloves garlic	2 crushed cloves garlic
½ teaspoon thyme	½ teaspoon thyme
½ teaspoon fennel	½ teaspoon fennel
1 tablespoon wholemeal flour	1 tablespoon whole wheat flour
½ pint (285ml) milk	1⅓ cups milk
5 fl oz (150ml) single cream	⅔ cup light cream
1 egg, beaten	1 egg, beaten
sea salt and black pepper	sea salt and black pepper
2 tablespoons wholemeal breadcrumbs	2 tablespoons whole wheat breadcrumbs

1

Slice the onions and cook them in boiling salted water about 4 minutes so that they are still a little crisp. Drain them well.

2

Heat the oil in a pan and add the garlic and herbs; cook a moment then add the flour, stirring so that the flour is cooked through. Slowly add the milk, stirring so that it forms a thick sauce. Pour in the cream and continue to stir. Season with salt and pepper.

3

Pour the onions into a shallow earthenware dish — the tian. Pour the sauce over the onions and scatter the breadcrumbs over the top. Bake in a preheated 375°F/190°C (Gas Mark 5) oven 20–30 minutes or until the top is crisp and brown.

FÈVES À LA POULETTE

Corsica

Imperial (Metric)	American
2 lb (900g) broad beans	2 pounds fava beans
1 oz (30g) butter	2½ tablespoons butter
1 teaspoon flour	1 teaspoon flour
sea salt and black pepper	sea salt and black pepper
2 egg yolks	2 egg yolks
1 tablespoon thick cream	1 tablespoon heavy cream
2 tablespoons chopped parsley	2 tablespoons chopped parsley

1

Shell the beans and cook them in a little water about 8 minutes; strain them, but keep about ¼ pint (150ml) of the water.

2

Melt the butter in a pan, stir in the flour and cook for a moment, then add the ¼ pint of water. Season with salt and black pepper and put the beans into the sauce. Let them cook a couple of minutes.

3

Stir in the egg yolks and then the cream; let the sauce thicken, then sprinkle with the chopped parsley.

POMMES DE TERRE À LA MÉRIDIONALE

France

Imperial (Metric)	American
1½ lb (680g) new potatoes	1½ pounds new potatoes
5 fl oz (150ml) olive oil	⅔ cup olive oil
10 cloves garlic, finely chopped	10 cloves garlic, finely chopped
sea salt and black pepper	sea salt and black pepper
3 tablespoons chopped parsley	3 tablespoons chopped parsley

1

Scrub the new potatoes and place them in a thick saucepan; pour in the olive oil and half the garlic and season generously with salt and pepper. Cover the pan and cook over gentle heat about 20 minutes.

2

When the potatoes are tender and golden brown take them out of the oil and place on a serving dish. Sprinkle with the rest of the garlic and all of the parsley.

NAVONI ALL'AGLIATA
Turnips with Garlic

Italy

Imperial (Metric)	American
1 lb (450g) turnips	1 pound turnips
5 tablespoons olive oil	5 tablespoons olive oil
sea salt and black pepper	sea salt and black pepper
4 crushed cloves garlic	4 crushed cloves garlic
1 tablespoon white wine vinegar	1 tablespoon white wine vinegar
2 tablespoons chopped parsley	2 tablespoons chopped parsley

1

Peel the turnips and simmer them in a little salted water 5 minutes. Drain and quarter them.

2

Heat the oil in a pan and sauté the turnips; season them with salt and pepper.

3

Mix the crushed garlic with vinegar and pour over the turnips as they are cooking. Raise the heat so that they become a little brown and crisp. They should be done within 5 minutes. Sprinkle with the parsley and serve.

CARROTS STEWED WITH RICE

Turkey

Imperial (Metric)	American
1 lb (450g) baby carrots	1 pound baby carrots
½ pint (285ml) olive oil	1⅓ cups olive oil
1 teaspoon each of crushed cumin and coriander	1 teaspoon each of crushed cumin and coriander
2 tablespoons brown rice	2 tablespoons brown rice
juice and zest of 1 lemon	juice and zest of 1 lemon
sea salt and black pepper	sea salt and black pepper
2 tablespoons chopped mint	2 tablespoons chopped mint

1

Cut the carrots in half lengthways, place them in a thick saucepan and pour the oil over them. Add the spices and the rice. Add the seasoning, lemon juice and zest. Pour in enough water just to cover.

2

Simmer them 40 minutes or until the rice is just cooked through. Place in a serving dish and sprinkle the mint over the top.

HARICOTS VERTS DE MONACO

Monaco

Imperial (Metric)	American
1 lb (450g) French beans	1 pound green beans
4 tablespoons olive oil	4 tablespoons olive oil
3 tomatoes, chopped	3 tomatoes, chopped
3 cloves garlic, chopped	3 cloves garlic, chopped
sea salt and black pepper	sea salt and black pepper

1
Trim the beans and cook in a little salted water about 10 minutes or until tender. Drain them well.

2
Heat the oil in a pan and add the chopped tomatoes and garlic. Stir to make a sauce; season well. Add the green beans and cook 3–5 minutes or until the tomatoes have amalgamated with the oil.

TOMATES À LA HUSSARDE
Stuffed Tomatoes

France

Imperial (Metric)	American
2 large tomatoes	2 large tomatoes
½ pint (185ml) soubise sauce (see page 159)	1⅓ cups soubise sauce (see page 159)
2 tablespoons freshly grated horseradish	2 tablespoons freshly grated horseradish

1

Cut the tomatoes in half and extract the flesh, leaving the empty shells. In a bowl mix the tomato pulp with the soubise sauce and horseradish; fill the tomatoes with the stuffing.

2

Bake in a preheated 400°F/200°C (Gas Mark 6) oven 15 minutes and to finish, brown under a hot grill (broiler).

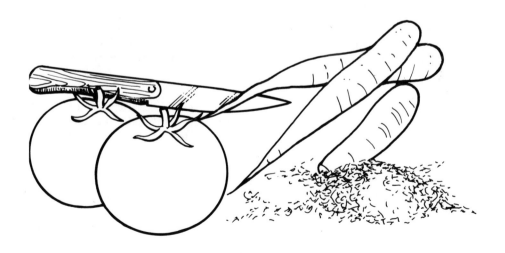

Chapter 9
Desserts, Fruits and Pastries

TURRÓN DE GUIRLACHE
Dark Almond Fudge

Spain

Imperial (Metric)	American
2 lb (900g) blanched almonds	8 cups blanched almonds
2 lb (900g) raw cane sugar	5⅓ cups raw cane sugar
juice of 1 lemon	juice of 1 lemon
1 tablespoon almond oil	1 tablespoon almond oil

1

Mix the lemon juice with the sugar in a pan and heat, stirring with a wooden spoon, until the sugar is dissolved. Add the almonds and continue to stir a few minutes.

2

Smear a flat baking tin with the almond oil and pour the mixture over the surface, levelling it out with the spoon to about ½ inch (6mm) in thickness.

3

Before it has hardened completely, mark out rectangles with a knife, cutting almost through to the base. Let it finally cool and harden.

TURRÓN DE JIJONA
Soft Almond Fudge

Spain

Imperial (Metric)	American
½ lb (225g) blanched almonds	2 cups blanched almonds
½ lb (225g) hazelnuts	2 cups hazelnuts
½ lb (225g) honey	1¼ cups honey
½ lb (225g) raw cane sugar	1⅓ cups raw cane sugar
5 egg whites	5 egg whites
1 tablespoon almond oil	1 tablespoon almond oil

1
Place the almonds and hazelnuts in a baking dish in a fairly hot oven 10 minutes until they are lightly toasted. When they are cool, put them in a blender and grind them coarsely.

2
Mix the honey and sugar and heat so the sugar dissolves. Pour in the nuts and cook 5 minutes, stirring all the time. Take away from the heat and let it cool.

3
Whip the egg whites until they are stiff and fold them into the mixture. Oil a baking tray and pour the mixture onto it and let it harden.

TORRIJAS
Cinnamon Bread with Honey

Spain

Imperial (Metric)	American
1 wholemeal loaf, sliced	1 whole wheat loaf, sliced
1 pint (570ml) milk	2½ cups milk
2 oz (55g) raw cane sugar	⅓ cup raw cane sugar
¼ pint (150ml) dry white wine	⅔ cup dry white wine
2 tablespoons brandy	2 tablespoons brandy
3 eggs, beaten	3 eggs, beaten
olive oil for sautéing	olive oil for sautéing
honey and cinnamon for	honey and cinnamon for
spreading on fried bread	spreading on fried bread

1
Soak the bread slices in a mixture of the milk, sugar, wine and brandy. Drain the bread and dip them in the beaten eggs, then fry in the olive oil until golden on both sides.

2
Drain on absorbent paper and serve coated with honey and sprinkled with cinnamon.

NATILLAS
Custard

Spain

Imperial (Metric)	American
2 eggs + 1 extra yolk	2 eggs + 1 extra yolk
4 oz (100g) raw cane sugar	⅔ cup raw cane sugar
1 teaspoon ground cinnamon	1 teaspoon ground cinnamon
¾ pint (425ml) milk	2 cups milk

1

Beat eggs, sugar and extra egg yolk together. Heat the milk with the cinnamon then pour in the eggs, stirring all the time over a low flame until the mixture thickens.

2

Pour into a serving dish and let it chill and set.

ESH ES SERAYA
Palace Bread

Egypt

Imperial (Metric)	American
$\frac{1}{2}$ lb (225g) honey	$\frac{2}{3}$ cup honey
4 oz (100g) raw cane sugar	$\frac{2}{3}$ cup raw cane sugar
4 oz (100g) butter	$\frac{1}{2}$ cup butter
5 oz (140g) fresh wholemeal breadcrumbs	$2\frac{1}{2}$ cups fresh whole wheat breadcrumbs

1

Mix all the ingredients in a saucepan and cook stirring all the time about 5 minutes.

2

Pour into a tart tin and let cool. When it is quite cold it can be cut into triangular portions. Serve with whipped cream.

YOGURT FRITTERS

Turkey

Imperial (Metric)	American
1 pint (570ml) yogurt	2½ cups yogurt
zest of 1 lemon	zest of 1 lemon
2 eggs	2 eggs
½ lb (225g) wholemeal flour	2 cups whole wheat flour
corn oil for sautéing	corn oil for sautéing
fine ground raw cane sugar for dusting	fine ground raw cane sugar for dusting

1

Mix the yogurt, lemon zest and eggs then add the flour, beating all the time.

2

Heat the oil and drop the batter in spoonful by spoonful. Turn them so that they become golden brown.

3

Drain them on absorbent paper then roll them in the sugar. These can be served with whipped cream.

DATE CAKES

Lebanon

Imperial (Metric)	American
1 lb (450g) stoned dates	1 pound pitted dates
4 oz (100g) walnuts	1 cup walnuts
4 oz (100g) butter	½ cup butter
6 oz (170g) wholemeal flour	½ cup whole wheat flour

1

Chop the dates and walnuts and mix them with half the butter and the flour. Form the mixture into small cakes about 1½ inches (4–5 cm) in diameter.

2

Melt the rest of the butter in a pan and sauté the cakes in it until brown on both sides. Serve hot with whipped cream.

FRUIT SALAD

Israel

Imperial (Metric)	American
1 large ripe avocado	1 large ripe avocado
juice and zest of 2 lemons	juice and zest of 2 lemons
3 oranges	3 oranges
4 oz (100g) mild cheese	¼ cup mild cheese
1 tablespoon chopped walnuts	1 tablespoon chopped walnuts
1 tablespoon raw cane sugar	1 tablespoon raw cane sugar
pinch of cinnamon	pinch of cinnamon

1

Peel, stone (pit) and chop the avocado, place in a bowl and pour the lemon juice and zest over it. Peel the oranges and carefully remove all the pith. Cut them into thin slices and add them to the avocado with their juices. Cut the cheese into cubes and add.

2

Now add the rest of the ingredients and chill before serving.

DRIED FRUIT COMPOTE

Tunisia

Imperial (Metric)	American
1 lb (450g) dried fruits (apricots, peaches, figs, prunes)	1 pound dried fruits (apricots, peaches, figs, prunes)
2 oz (55g) raw cane sugar	⅓ cup raw cane sugar
juice and zest of 1 lemon	juice and zest of 1 lemon
1 oz (30g) chopped walnuts	3 tablespoons chopped walnuts

1
Soak the dried fruit overnight. In the morning bring the water and the fruit to a boil, add the sugar and simmer until the fruit is soft. Add the lemon juice and zest.

2
Pour into a serving bowl and sprinkle with the chopped nuts. Serve chilled with whipped cream.

FROMAGE BLANC AUX RAISINS SEC

France

Imperial (Metric)	American
½ lb (225g) fromage blanc	1 cup fromage blanc (soft white cheese)
1 oz (30g) muscatel raisins	3 tablespoons muscatel raisins
5 fl oz (150ml) brandy	⅔ cup brandy
juice and zest of 1 lemon	juice and zest of 1 lemon
1 oz (30g) raw cane sugar	2 tablespoons raw cane sugar
pinch of cinnamon	pinch of cinnamon

1

Soak the raisins in the brandy half a day. Add the lemon juice and zest, sugar and cinnamon.

2

Simmer the brandy mixture about 10 minutes then let it cool. Add it to the fromage blanc, beating it in, then pour into individual glasses.

MELON AUX RAISINS
Melon and Grapes

France

Imperial (Metric)	American
2 ogen melons	2 ogen melons
zest and juice of 2 lemons	zest and juice of 2 lemons
1 lb (450g) seedless grapes	1 pound seedless grapes
2 tablespoons fine raw cane sugar	2 tablespoons fine raw cane sugar

1

Quarter the melons, peel and discard the seeds, cut into chunks and place in a bowl. Cover with the zest and lemon juice.

2

Take the grapes from the stalks and strew them over the melon. Sprinkle with the sugar, chill and serve.

FLAN AUX MARRONS
Chestnut Custard

France

Imperial (Metric)	American
$\frac{1}{2}$ lb (225g) fresh or tinned chestnuts	$\frac{1}{2}$ pound fresh or canned chestnuts
4 eggs	4 eggs
2 oz (55g) raw cane sugar	$\frac{1}{3}$ cup raw cane sugar
$\frac{3}{4}$ pint (425ml) milk	2 cups milk
3 tablespoons dark rum	3 tablespoons dark rum

For the caramel

Imperial (Metric)	American
3 oz (85g) raw cane sugar	$\frac{1}{2}$ cup raw cane sugar
2 fl. oz (60ml) water	$\frac{1}{4}$ cup water

1
Heat the sugar in the water to make the caramel, simmer until it turns a dark chocolate colour and immediately pour into a cake tin, angling so that the caramel coats the sides and bottom; leave it to set.

2
If using fresh chestnuts, peel them and boil them in salted water 20 minutes. If using canned chestnuts, drain them thoroughly. Chop the chestnuts finely. Preheat the oven to 350°F/180°C (Gas Mark 4).

3
Beat the eggs with the sugar and mix in the milk and rum. Pour the mixture into the caramel-lined tin and place in a water bath. Ensure that the water is at the boiling point when it is placed in the oven.

4
After it has been cooking about 12 minutes, drop in the chopped chestnuts. Continue to cook another 25 minutes or until the custard is set. Leave to cool, then unmould.

TARTE AU CITRON
Lemon Tart

France

For the Pastry

Imperial (Metric)	American
½ lb (225g) wholemeal flour	2 cups whole wheat flour
4 egg yolks	4 egg yolks
½ teaspoon salt	½ teaspoon salt
2 oz (55g) raw cane sugar	⅓ cup raw cane sugar
3 drops vanilla essence	3 drops vanilla extract
4 oz (100g) butter, softened	½ cup butter, softened

For the filling

Imperial (Metric)	American
2 eggs	2 eggs
2 oz (55g) raw cane sugar	⅓ cup raw cane sugar
zest and juice of 2 lemons	zest and juice of 2 lemons
4 oz (100g) butter, melted	½ cup butter, melted
2 oz (55g) ground almonds	½ cup ground almonds

1

Butter an 11–12 inch (approx. 30cm) pie tin, then make the pastry. Sift the flour, make a well in the centre and put in the egg yolks, salt, sugar and vanilla and mix well. Add the butter to make a paste, work the dough for a few minutes and then chill 1 hour.

2

Roll out the dough and line the pie tin to make a pastry shell. Bake blind in a hot 425°F/220°C (Gas Mark 7) oven 10–12 minutes.

3

Make the filling by beating the eggs and the sugar then stir in the lemon juice, zest and melted butter followed by the ground almonds.

4

Place the pie tin on a hot baking sheet and pour the mixture into the pastry shell. Bake 30 minutes at 375°F/190°C (Gas Mark 5). Serve when warm.

FIGUES FRAICHES AU JUS D'ORANGE
Fresh Figs and Orange Juice

France

Imperial (Metric)	American
10 or 12 fresh figs	10 or 12 fresh figs
juice of 2 oranges	juice of 2 oranges

1

Cut off stalks then quarter the figs. Lay them in a large glass bowl and pour the orange juice over them. Let them marinate in the juice a few hours before serving.

CRÈME DE NOIX ET MIÈL
Honey and Walnut Cream

France

Imperial (Metric)	American
3 oz (85g) chopped walnuts	$\frac{2}{3}$ cup chopped walnuts
5 fl oz (150ml) honey	$\frac{2}{3}$ cup honey
1 pint (570ml) thick cream	$2\frac{1}{2}$ cups heavy cream

1

Grind half of the walnuts to a powder and leave the rest coarsely chopped. Add them to the honey and both to the thick cream, beat and mix well.

2

Pour into individual glasses and chill well before serving.

MACEDONIA DI FRUTTA
Fresh Fruit Salad

Italy

Imperial (Metric)	American
1 ogen melon, peeled, seeded, and cut into chunks	1 ogen melon, peeled, seeded and cut into chunks
2 lb (900g) assorted fruit (pears, peaches, cherries, grapes, plums, figs, apples) stoned and cut into cubes	2 pounds assorted fruit (pears, peaches, cherries, grapes, plums, figs, apples) pitted and cut into cubes
2 oz (55g) raw cane sugar	⅓ cup raw cane sugar
juice of 1 lemon and 2 oranges	juice of 1 lemon and 2 oranges

1

Put all the cubed fruit into a large glass bowl, sprinkle with sugar and pour the fruit juice over it all.

2

Chill several hours.

PESCA CON VINO ROSSO
Peaches in Red Wine

Italy

Imperial (Metric)	American
6 large ripe peaches	6 large ripe peaches
2 tablespoons raw cane sugar	2 tablespoons raw cane sugar
1 pint (570ml) red wine	2½ cups red wine

1

Peel the peaches and slice them into a large bowl.

2

Sprinkle them with the sugar and pour enough wine over them just to cover. If any is left over, drink it!

TORRONE MOLLE
Chocolate Nut Dessert

Italy

Imperial (Metric)	American
½ lb. (225g) unsalted butter, softened	1 cup unsalted butter, softened
½ lb (225g) raw cane sugar	1⅓ cups raw cane sugar
4 oz (100g) cocoa	1 cup cocoa
1 egg and 1 egg yolk	1 egg and 1 egg yolk
4 oz (100g) almonds, coarsely chopped	¾ cup almonds, coarsely chopped
2 oz (55g) walnuts, coarsely chopped	⅓ cup walnuts, coarsely chopped
3 tablespoons dark rum	3 tablespoons dark rum

1
Mix the butter and sugar together in a bowl so that you have a cream. Add the cocoa and allow the cream to absorb it gradually.

2
Beat the egg and egg yolk and add to the cream. Then add the rest of the ingredients. Mix well.

3
Line a loaf tin with buttered greaseproof paper, pour the mixture into it, smooth it down and chill overnight. Before serving, unmould.

PERE ALLA CREMA DEL LAGO DI COMO
Stewed Pears in Grappa Cream

Italy

Imperial (Metric)	American
4 pears	4 pears
juice and zest of 1 lemon	juice and zest of 1 lemon
1 oz (30g) raw cane sugar	2 tablespoons raw cane sugar
3 fl oz (85ml) grappa	⅓ cup grappa or other fiery brandy
½ pint (285ml) double cream	1⅓ cups heavy cream

For the syrup

Imperial (Metric)	American
4 oz (100g) raw cane sugar	⅔ cup raw cane sugar
8 fl oz (225ml) water	1 cup water

1
Make a syrup by dissolving the sugar in the water over gentle heat. Peel the pears, slice them in half and core them. Cook the pears in the syrup about 8 minutes or until just tender.

2
Dissolve the sugar with the juice and zest of the lemon in the grappa by heating it gently; let it cool.

3
Whip the cream until it is stiff and fold the liqueur mixture into it. Lift the pears out of the syrup, arrange them in a large bowl and cover with the cream. Chill 2 or 3 hours before serving.

CREMA ALLA MASCARPONE

Italy

Imperial (Metric)	American
2 eggs	2 eggs
2 oz (55g) raw cane sugar	⅔ cup raw cane sugar
½ lb (225g) Mascarpone cheese	1 cup Mascarpone cheese

1

Separate the eggs and beat the sugar into the egg yolks. Add the Mascarpone cheese and beat until you have a smooth mixture.

2

Whip the egg whites until they are stiff then fold these into the creamed cheese. Serve in individual glasses.

PESCHE RIPIENE
Stuffed Peaches

Italy

Imperial (Metric)	American
5 ripe peaches	5 ripe peaches
juice and zest of 2 lemons	juice and zest of 2 lemons
1 oz (25g) raw cane sugar	2 tablespoons raw cane sugar
2 oz (55g) ground almonds	$\frac{1}{2}$ cup ground almonds
2 macaroons	2 macaroons
5 fl oz (145ml) white wine	$\frac{2}{3}$ cup white wine

1
Plunge the peaches into boiling water for a moment and then skin them, cut them in half and remove the stones.

2
Place one peach in a blender and reduce to a pulp; add the lemon juice and zest, sugar, almonds and macaroons, blend to a smooth paste with the wine.

3
Butter a baking dish and place the peaches in it, their cut sides uppermost, spoon the stuffing into them. Bake for 30 minutes at 350°F/180°C (Gas Mark 4).

INDEX

254